THE THERAPIST AS LISTENER

Peter Wilberg

THE THERAPIST AS
LISTENER

**MARTIN HEIDEGGER AND THE MISSING DIMENSION
OF COUNSELLING AND PSYCHOTHERAPY TRAINING**

New Gnosis Publications

First published by **New Gnosis Publications**
www.newgnosis.co.uk

Printed and bound in England by Antony Rowe Ltd
Distributed by Gardners Books, Eastbourne, Sussex

ISBN 1-904519-05-9

"You cannot heal a single human being, even with psychotherapy, if you do not first restore his relationship to Being."

Martin Heidegger

CONTENTS

PREFACE

Counselling and psychotherapy, like many other forms of professional practice are based on a specific framework of practical relations between the professional and his or her clients. Similarly, training in counselling and psychotherapy, like that in other professions involving one-to-one relationships to the client, focuses on the knowledge and skills necessary to pursue a successful *practical relation* with the client. Herein lies a fundamental paradox however. For counselling and psychotherapy are essentially *relational practices*. As such, they cannot be reduced to a set of *practical relations* and the professional knowledge and practices that shape these relations.

Despite the lip-service paid to the importance of the 'therapeutic relationship', the very *term* obscures this distinction between a therapist's professionalised practical relations to their clients on the one hand, and their personal relational practices, on the other. We would be better off speaking not of some 'thing' called the therapeutic *relationship* but rather asking ourselves what constitutes therapeutic *relating*? A simple answer would be *listening*. One might think that listening - understood as a relational practice - would be *the* central focus of *all* forms of psychotherapy and counselling training (not to mention medical training). The fact that it is not is testament to a general 'psychopathology' of human relations to which the counselling and therapeutic 'relationship' can too easily fall prey. This general pathology - which affects each and every client - is the subordination of relational practices to institutionalised social and professional practices of all sorts.

The primary aim of the essays and articles collected in this book is to emphasise the intrinsically therapeutic character of *listening* - understood as a *relational practice* and not merely as the application of a body of theoretical knowledge and professional 'skills' to the 'therapeutic relationship'. Above all it is the thinking of Martin Heidegger that allows us to understand listening not just as a 'communication skill' but as a fundamental mode of human being or *Dasein* - that of *being with others* (*Mitsein*). Listening as a *relational practice* is a practice of being with others in silence which requires the listener to be both fully 'there' (*Da-sein*) and to be fully *with* the other (*Mit-sein*). Yet being fully *there* and *with* the other requires not just the professional attention or personal empathy of the listener but their *fully embodied presence* as a human being. For it is only by listening with and from their whole body that the therapist can listen with and from their whole being and in this way be both fully there (*Da*) and 'all ear'. I understand listening therefore not simply as a relational practice but as a *bodily relational practice* - a relational activity of our whole body and whole being and not just the instrumental professional use of our ears and minds.

As for the innately *therapeutic* power of listening as a relational practice, I believe this lies essentially in its *maieutic* character (from the Greek *maieuesthai* - 'to act as a midwife'). Listening - being with oneself and others in pregnant silence - is the *midwife* of speech. What I call 'maieutic listening' however, is a specific mode of not only being but *bearing with* others in the pregnancy of silence. Only such a therapeutic bearing can help another to not only 'endure' their own suffering but bear and body it - allowing it to give birth to a new *inner bearing* towards the world and other beings.

The chapters of this book have been compiled from independent essays or articles written over a period of ten years - during which time my own understanding and articulation of listening has naturally undergone its own changes and refinements. Though written at different times, from somewhat different angles and with some variation in discourse style, all the chapters argue that the phenomenology of listening is a fundamental, missing dimension of psychotherapy and counselling training. They also argue for a fundamental shift in the primary focus of psychotherapy and counselling as such - from the pathology of the client (in whatever way this is theoretically understood) to the relational practices of the therapist *as listener*. This in turn requires a shift in focus from specific psychological states and processes that a client may present and be *aware of* to an attunement (*Einstimmung*) on the part of the therapist or counsellor with those felt tonalities *of awareness* that tune and tone (*bestimmen*) the client's whole way of being in the world.

Feeling tones and 'fundamental moods' (*Grundstimmungen*) are not psychic contents in themselves and yet they colour an individual's whole way of experiencing themselves and others. They are also the very wavelengths of attunement linking practitioner and client and as such 'carrier waves' of messages which communicate directly to the client. The fundamental message of this book is that listening is itself an active form of silent inner communication with others. For the mode and manner in which we listen to another human being - above all the inwardly felt *tone* of our listening - is something that directly communicates, bearing back or 're-lating' its own message *to* the other, and telling them - even before they speak - how we see them and to what extent we are open to truly hearing them. It is in this sense that listening is in itself a relational practice and therefore also an *ethical* practice in the deepest sense.

In stark contrast to this message is the belief - so entrenched and taken for granted that it is almost invisible - that listening is a mere *prelude* to some form of verbal response or therapeutic intervention on the part of the counsellor or therapist. This belief ignores the intrinsically communicative character and potentially therapeutic character of listening as such. Instead of thinking of listening as a prelude to finding their *own* response to a client's words, counsellors and therapists need to constantly remind themselves that what a client reveals to them in the counselling or therapy session, along with the manner in which they reveal it, is already and in itself *a response* to the inner bearing of the counsellor or therapist *as listener.*

BEING AND LISTENING

Philosophical Counselling as Listening Dialogue

Introduction

The unity of 'being and listening' was nowhere better affirmed than in a quintessential maxim of Martin Heidegger:

> '*We* hear, not the ear.'

He goes on to say:

'... if we hear, something is not merely added to what the ear picks up; rather, what the ear perceives and how it perceives will already be attuned (*gestimmt*) and determined (*bestimmt*) by what we hear ...'

Such a 'language of listening', with its roots in a German vocabulary, is one that many have not heard before - and when they do hear it find difficult to follow. It will have an unfamiliar ring to those whose understanding of the counselling relationship is led by terminologies derived from Freud or Rogers, or from 'cognitive-behavioural', 'psychodynamic' and 'integrative' psychologies. The object of this work is to begin to show the as yet unheard significance of this vocabulary, not in the narrow context of academic philosophy and Heidegger scholarship, but in a much wider human context. For it possesses, I believe, a power to radically deepen our experience of listening, and thereby to transform our whole understanding of 'inter-personal communication'.

'Questioning' and 'Questing'

Philosophy, as we know it from Plato's Socrates is a dialogue and a process of questioning. So is counselling. In both forms of dialogue questions are stated and explored without being finally answered. Both the philosopher and the counsellor also listen for questions that are unstated and merely implied. Many of the unstated and unexplored questions raised in philosophical dialogues are personal ones. They are not propositions to be argued but concern the philosopher's personal inner relationship to what is being talked about. Conversely, many of the unstated and implicit questions raised in counselling dialogues are philosophical ones - they brook no easy answer because they are not problems to be solved but questions to be experienced - questions that we all live. The historical relation between philosophy and counselling is the relation between philosophy and life - it has to do essentially with the relation between stated and unstated questions, questions that are asked in words and questions that are personally lived, that are posed and answered by life.

The questions we confront in our lives are more than just personal or psychological questions. Instead they are always rooted in shared 'philosophical' questions of existence - 'pre-personal', 'inter-personal' or 'trans-personal' - that address both counsellor and client. No counsellor or therapist can answer a client's questions. Nor can counsellors dissociate themselves from these questions as if they were the private property of the client. Clients often come to counselling not just because they face difficult questions, nor even because they feel alone in dealing with these questions, but because they feel it is their question alone. The underlying question they address to the counsellor is 'Am I the only person experiencing this problem?' The answer is always yes and no. Yes, because we each confront and respond to fundamental life questions in a different way. No, because underneath all issues relating to our personal psychological responses to life's challenges remain questions which we all share - questions which are 'philosophical' not because they are abstract but because they are living questions - part of the very fabric of life. If this is not fully recognised, our compassion for a person's problems and suffering, our very skill in helping them to see new emotional or practical aspects of the questions they face, can implicitly add to the client's sense of being the question's sole bearer. Most people come to counselling not out of a full awareness of the questions facing them but out of an awareness that, whatever problem it is that confronts them, there is some felt question lurking within it that they have not yet found or asked themselves. That is to say, they are not groping for an answer so much as groping for the question. The counsellor may be aware that questions a client raises in relation to their 'presenting' problems only skim the surface, and yet the client may cling to these questions for fear of being totally in the dark without them.

A question we are in the dark about is a situation or condition (social, physical or psychological) that lingers and 'nags us' despite all our attempts to reduce it to a superficial practical question or to respond to it - answer it - in our habitual ways. Nagged or oppressed by a felt question in this way we do not feel fully ourselves, and instead feel the question as a sense of being apart from ourselves. The more profound question - the philosophical question as opposed to the presenting question - is not essentially psychological in nature. It does not have to do with our infantile or childhood past or even our existential future. It is not a question 'about' anything practical, nor is it a question 'about' an existential theme such as death, freedom, meaning, values, etc. The philosophical question is the question that we experience wordlessly - it is the very sense of apartness from our own being and other beings that nags or oppresses us through the presenting problem. It is a question not of what we experience but of how and whom we experience ourselves to be - a question of being. Not a question we 'have' but a question that 'has us' - that expresses a felt rift in our very being.

The verbal questions that we pose to ourselves are false not because they are irrelevant or unimportant. They may be extremely important. They are false in so far as they can only be answered by first surrendering to the fundamental question - the underlying sense of apartness from ourselves and the negative relation to ourselves that goes along with this - our negative feelings towards the situation we are in, and how it makes us feel. Surrendering to the fundamental question as a question of being means acknowledging the reality of our situation - not what it is but that it is. It also means acknowledging that we do not merely 'have' a problem but that in essence we are the problem. The apartness we feel from ourselves as a result of the problem, and our inability to fully be ourselves in the face of this problem, is the problem.

To allow ourselves to be the question, to acknowledge this apartness from ourselves, is painful. Or rather what we call 'pain' is this very sense of apartness from our own being, whether experienced through a physical or psychological condition. A question is painful because it demands an unconditional surrender of all our previous questions and answers. To abandon our superficial questions however, is not the same as abandoning all hope of an answer. Quite the contrary, for by 'being the question' we turn our mental and verbal questioning into an authentic questing of our being. In turn, we open ourselves to receiving an answer from our own being.

The moment we allow ourselves to be the question we begin to become the answer - for we begin to acknowledge all those aspects of ourselves that we have hitherto kept at a distance by objectifying them in the form of an outer or inner 'problem'. The moment the question becomes fully and wholly a question of being is the moment we begin again to become whole as beings - to heal. This healing or becoming whole, no longer feeling apart from ourselves, is the fundamental change that allows us to receive new answers to our surface questions - answers that are authentic because they arise from a transformation of our being. Or to put this in slightly different terms - by questing with our being we open ourselves to receiving an answering call from our being, whether in the form of an insight, a chance event or opportunity, an expansion of perspective or a spontaneous sense of relief, a lightening of our burden.

The burden of a problem is like the burden of a pregnancy. We carry or bear the question that we have not yet answered as a burden that we cannot alleviate by merely talking about it. Physical symptoms, no less than psychological distress, are both a form of pregnancy. What is pregnant in both is a transformation of our self-being. This need for transformation may be experienced as distress (in fact the German word for 'need' is the same as that for 'distress' - *Not*). What precipitated or seeded the pregnancy is one thing. Attempts to accelerate or abort it are another. 'Being the question' allows us to bear and body it as a form of pregnancy, and in this way to give birth to a new inner bearing or disposition - to 'become the answer'.

'A disposition can confine man in his corporeality as in a prison. Yet it can also carry him through corporeality as one of the paths leading out of it.'

Martin Heidegger

Presuppositions of Counselling - identity as private property

All experience is both experience of something other than self (a thing, person, situation or event) and self-experience (something that colours our experience of ourselves). What we experience, inwardly or outwardly, always impinges to some extent on our self-experience - on who we experience ourselves to be. Yet the linguistic ego - the word 'I' - constantly reinforces the notion of a self that remains unchanged by its own experiences. The very structure of language implies a subject separate and immune from its own verbs and objects - as if my self-experience when 'I' (subject) engage in the activity of listening (verb) to music (object) were the same as when 'I' fill in a tax return form. By separating self-experience into two parts, an unchanging 'I' and the (changing) experiences that this 'I' has, language transforms our self-being into a fixed sense of personal identity represented by the linguistic ego. Conversely, it is through the linguistic 'I' that we sustain a fixed sense of identity, preventing what we experience from affecting and altering our *self-experience*. By splitting self-experience into self + experience, language also separates self-experience from our experience of others and otherness. In this way it transforms experience and identity into the private experiential property of persons - 'I' and 'you', 'him' and 'her', 'us' and 'them'. This creates a rift between language and being, one that makes rifts in our own self-being appear as rifts between persons, between self and other. It is this rift between language and being that makes us see our problems as 'personal' ones only rather than as questions of being.

The value of philosophy for counselling is to introduce a language of being that overcomes the notion of identity as private property. Nowhere in the current language of counselling, however, do we find a language of being. Instead we find a language of personal and inter-personal boundaries. The philosophical assumption here is that boundaries are what *separate* individuals and families, counties and cultures, and that therefore two individuals, like two countries, can either maintain their boundaries or merge to become one. This assumption goes together with the belief that the function of the counsellor's role 'boundaries' is to separate their own experience from that of the client, to 'own' their identity as private property and help clients to do the same. In responding to the questions facing their clients counsellors will of course draw on their own life experience. Indeed they will tend to attract clients for whom this experience is particularly valuable. By sharing their experience in this way, even if only indirectly, they acknowledge a level at which all experience is experience of something shared and all questions are shared questions. As we have seen however, even compassion and insight can be isolating to the client, if the basic inner stance of the counsellor is not a philosophical one in this sense - does not acknowledge essential questions and dimensions of experience as shared ones. 'Psychologising' becomes a substitute for the philosophical recognition of those deeper questions of human being, all of which are shared questions and none are finally 'resolved'. Such 'philosophical' questions are not merely questions for philosophers. They are questions lived by every human being as a basic *questing* for meaning in their lives. Such lived questions are 'quest-ions'.

Solving existential or emotional problems is not the same thing as answering fundamental questions - questions of being. Psychological problems are questions that are experienced as personally painful because they bring to light a rift within our own being. And yet the questing of our being for wholeness is never finally resolved. This is why, although insight into different psychological or practical aspects of a question helps people to solve their problems (and in this way to make their experience of these questions less 'painful') it does not answer those questions as questions of being - as 'quest-ions'.

Questions may become more painful than necessary by seeing them merely as problems to be solved - the temptation of the client, or believing that in answering questions one has resolved the fundamental questing of our being that underlies them - the temptation of the counsellor. To do so is to foreclose the more fundamental quest-ions, leading to the *hubris* of imagining oneself to have 'solved' them, or to an unnecessary sense of inferiority arising from feeling that one has not yet done so whereas others have.

There is a difference, then, between solving problems and believing that in solving these problems one has resolved the underlying quest-ions. This difference comes to life when a client's problems raise issues that seem 'coincidentally' to be very 'close to home' - that mirror current and unresolved problems in the counsellor's own life. It is then that the latter may feel inadequate or destabilised in their role boundaries, afraid of 'counter-transference' or of 'projecting' their own feelings onto the client. This is one expression of a basic paradox. For the more we seek to separate our own experience from that of others the more insecure our boundaries become.

Shared quest-ions are like shared boundaries - on one side is my response to the quest, on another side is yours. These responses are what distinguishes us as human beings. Yet they are also what draws us together in a common quest. It is by staying with the question as a common quest-ion that we both acknowledge the shared dimension of all questions - their shared reality as 'questions of being' - and at the same time distinguish ourselves as beings. The questions posed by a counsellor do not simply mirror the questing of the client or meet their request for support and assistance. They also express the questing of the counsellor - their own ongoing quest for meaning and the quest-ions this raises for them.

Letting go of surface questions may seem to both counsellor and client like a form of resignation. When we become aware of a gap between language and being we either become speechless or escape into verbal curiosity - what Heidegger called 'idle talk'. Wordlessness is a withdrawal from idle talk and superficial language. It is often seen and experienced as a symptom of depression. The retreat from superficial language and questions may seem like an act of resignation - giving up our life-quest and our quest for life. And yet it is this very retreat that allows us once again to wordlessly experience the questing of our being for wholeness and meaning, and with patience to find words for our own quest-ions, not dead words but living words. In philosophy and in counselling one question leads to another. The question is whether they lead us away from or towards our own being.

Questing is what we do when we allow ourselves to be the question. In music, a single note or chord might tremble with a certain incompleteness and in this sense quest a response from an answering chord or note. There are no verbal questions and answers in a piece of music, and yet we hear in its tones a constant questing and response. The same is true of the music of feeling. It is through tones of feeling that we quest an answering response, not in words but from answering tones that communicate *dia-logos*: not in but *through* the word.

Towards a Philosophy of Listening - 'empathy' and 'attunement'

Like questions, feelings too are not essentially the *private property* of persons. They are tones of being - shared wavelengths of attunement that connect us to our own being and at the same time link and join one being with another. They are 'boundaries' that join. If a counsellor tells a client that 'I detect some fear in you' this implies that the counsellor either identifies a signal of the client as an indication of fear, or that she herself 'senses' this fear - feels it to some extent herself. The capacity to identify a verbal or body signal as a signal *of* something does not necessarily imply a capacity to either *identify* or fully identify *with* what is behind that signal. The very language of the statement 'I detect some fear in you' is a language of emotional *dis-identification*. 'I' only 'detect' this 'fear', which is essentially 'in you'. Identification on the other hand, implies a capacity to identify with and thereby feel the feelings of another - in which case they cease to be merely the *other's feelings* - their private emotional property. Emotion words such as 'fear', 'anger', 'sadness' imply that these emotions are things-in-themselves rather than ways of experiencing and expressing particular felt qualities of awareness that we sense in ourselves and others. The expression 'I detect some fear in you' turns the fear not only into something that is the private property of the client, a 'thing-in-itself' independent of the counsellor's own personal experience and expression of it. The counsellor regards herself as having picked up or empathised with the client's fear rather than as having felt something that she herself interprets - verbally and experientially - as a thing called 'fear'.

It is by translating our feelings into nameable emotions belonging to persons that they become private emotional property - 'mine' or 'yours', 'his' or 'hers'. The structures of language constantly translate what goes on between human beings into something going on 'in' persons - 'in' me or 'in' you, 'in' him or 'in' her. In describing our feelings in these terms we fail to question and understand the language of emotional discourse philosophically - to take a stand under and beneath this language and its structures. To do so means attuning our listening not so much to what is going on 'in' people as to what is going on 'between' them - going on in that common and essential space of the 'interhuman' or *Zwischenmenschliche* (Martin Buber) that is often translated simply as 'the between'. For the philosophical counsellor it is this common space of the interhuman to which each human being most essentially *belongs*. The German word for 'belonging' is *Zu-gehörigkeit* - quite literally a 'hearing together'. This hearing together is also a belonging together because it is a hearing capable of elongating and enduring the temporal intervals of shared silence without which no individual in a group can feel themselves dwelling in the common space of the interhuman - the 'between' to which all belong.

'To hear what is silent requires a hearing that each of us has and no-one uses correctly. This hearing (*Gehör*) has something to do not only with the ear, but also with a human's belonging (*Zugehörigkeit*) to what its essence is attuned to. Humans are at-tuned (*ge-stimmt*) to what de-termines (*be-stimmt*) their essence. In this attunement humans are touched and called forth by a voice (*Stimme*) that peals all the more purely, the more it silently reverberates through what speaks.'

Martin Heidegger

13

Relationality is determined by our attunement (*Einstimmung*) with another being. The German word for 'determine' is *bestimmen*, related, like *Einstimmung* to the word *Stimme* (voice) and *Stimmung* (mood or feeling tone). The formal meaning of *bestimmen* is to determine or to destine - to 'hold sway' over. Its essential meaning is something like 'to set a tone'. The way we silently attune to another person sets a tone, which determines or holds sway over how we perceive them. This does not mean that our perceptions are mere 'projections'. For if they were, we would not be 'tuned in' at all. It is precisely because we are tuned in and not merely projecting that we can also tune the wavelength of that attunement - as we do on a radio receiver. Feeling tones are the silent carrier waves on which a listener not only receives but also transmits messages to a speaker - wordlessly relaying their *listening response*.

Someone may tune into a radio music station and describe the music that they hear as 'fearful'. Another person may describe it quite differently. Both descriptions are translations of something essentially wordless - music - and something that we hear only because we have tuned into it, set a certain 'frequency' or 'wavelength' of attunement. Musical tones only speak to us if we really attune to them with our feelings - if we let them echo our feeling tones. We only really listen to music when we listen through the music to ourselves - for it is by attuning to it with feeling that it recalls us to our being.

The feeling tones with which we attune to someone not only allow us to hear the music of their feelings - they recall us to our own being and echo its 'toning'. How a counsellor hears and responds to another person's feelings therefore always has to do with the music they are playing - the tone and tune of their listening attunement (*Einstimmung*). It also has to do with their own language - how they interpret, experience and *experientially interpret* these feeling tones in emotional terms.

The term 'emotional empathy' is itself a substitute for a philosophy of listening and feeling that explores the inner nature of 'attunement' and 'rapport'. Given the proliferation of theories and schools of counselling it is surprising that there has not yet been any attempt to formulate a depth philosophy or psychology of listening. For despite its obvious centrality to psychotherapy and psychoanalysis the very word 'listening' is rarely found in the literature on psychotherapy and counselling. In the psychoanalytic literature a deep philosophy and psychology of listening is replaced by theoretical 'listening perspectives' - conceptual frameworks for interpreting what the analysand says. In counselling literature and training the focus is at best only on listening 'skills'. At their worst these have to do not with listening at all but only with the use of body language and verbal mirroring to give a client the outward *impression* of being listened to and truly heard. Throughout the literature the fundamental question of what listening as such essentially *is* is never asked. As a result, the question of what it means to truly listen to another - and not merely interpret what is heard or give another the comforting appearance of being listened to - is foreclosed right from the start.

The 'Psychology' of Listening - Heraclitus

Heraclitus wrote: 'You will not find out the limits of the *psyche* by going around it, so deep is its *logos*.' It is therefore the greatest arrogance to think that it is only in modern 'psychology' that the first attempt was made to understand the nature and truth of the psyche and of its 'speech' or *logos*. It was no modern psychologist but the 'philosopher' Heraclitus who was the first true 'psycho-logist'. For he was the first thinker to conjoin the Greek words *psyche* and *logos* and say something of their relation. For Heraclitus, the *logos* of the psyche meant something like an inner resonance or reverberation, a reverberation or 'report' so deep we can never trace it by 'going around it' - by *circumscribing* its surface in language. Heraclitus understood the deep *logos* of the *psyche* as that which preceded all ordinary human speaking and listening - which is why he could suggest that 'men fail to comprehend it, both before hearing and once they have heard', for 'not knowing how to listen, neither can they speak.' The Stoic philosophers who followed him distinguished between the outer word (*logos prophorikos*) and its wordless source and inner resonance - the 'inner word' or *logos endiathetos*. Language is a vehicle for giving expression to the outer word. Yet it was not the outer word or *logos prophorikos* that Heraclitus was referring to when he said:

'Although this *logos* is shared, most men live as
though their sensibility were a private possession.'

The way we translate this *logos* into words shapes the way we fulfil
and realise our being in worldly terms. Wording is 'worlding' - the
way we shape our own experience in word and deed, and through it
create our personal reality. A language governed by verbal polarities
of whatever sort - 'success' vs. 'failure', 'joy' vs. 'pain', 'high' vs.
'low', 'intellect' vs. 'emotion', 'transference' vs. 'counter-transference',
'counselling' vs. 'philosophy', 'speaking' vs. 'listening' - creates a
life-world governed by these polarities. Only our listening can
transcend these verbal polarities. Thought itself is an oscillation
between this outer and inner logos, between words and the wordless
resonances of the psyche. This oscillation has its own inner sound
and its own meaning - its own tone and intentionality. The problem
today is that we identify thinking only with verbally articulated
thoughts. The *logos* of Heraclitus has long since been reduced to a
multiplicity of scientific '-ologies' such as *bio-logy, socio-logy,
psycho-logy*, etc. reduced in philosophy to 'logical' reasoning and in
society to military and commercial 'logistics' and the 'logo'.

In analytic philosophy to 'listen to the *logos*' has been reduced to
listening for 'logical' contradictions in verbal propositions - not to
the unstated, implicit or 'inner' word. 'Dialogue' amongst academic
and analytic philosophers actually demands no listening and involves
no dialogue at all - no listening to what seeks to communicate itself
through the word (*dia-logos*). In academic discourse, deep
philosophical dialogue - *listening dialogue* - has long since been
reduced to a mere cultivated sport of intellectual point-scoring.

As a result, the wordless dimension of thinking has been lost not
only to science but to philosophy. Psychoanalysis acknowledges this
dimension of thinking through the concept of the 'unconscious' but
does so using 'psychological' terminologies that are themselves
based primarily on verbal reasoning, interpretation and 'logic'. As a
result there is a confusion of competing theories and terminologies,
none of which reclaim their linguistic roots and the *etymos logos* -
the truth (*etymos*) of the word (*logos*). By listening to language
philosophically we can re-link meanings that words have divided and
polarised.

Heidegger heard in the Greek word *logos* an echo of the related Greek verb *legein* - to gather. This echo can still be heard in the English expression 'I gather'. Listening is *legein* - a gathering of impressions. 'Listen to the logos' means attending to what is gathering within us - letting it ripen and mature before seeking to harvest it in words or mental pictures. Even to describe what gathers in terms of nameable emotions or thoughts, or to challenge it forth with questions, however 'open', can give premature birth to the *logos prophorikos* and foreclose our listening. And yet this is exactly what much counselling practice encourages by its emphasis on verbal echoing, mirroring, summarising and questioning. Most training in so-called listening skills is based on a negative definition of listening - not interrupting, not giving advice, not answering questions for the client etc. There is no *positive* understanding of the essence of listening as *legein* - a wordless attunement that patiently and meditatively 'gathers' the felt inner sense, resonance and essence of what has been said.

Philosophy in Heraclitus's sense did not mean 'talking philosophy' but listening philosophically. Philosophy and counselling are both rooted in listening - meditative listening. Neither involve simply asking or answering questions. Both involve hearing and responding to the unstated and shared questions implied by people's words. Hearkening to the wordless questing of each other's being. Meditative listening is not questioning but questing. It is the way we attend questingly to language, to being, and to speaking beings - human beings. 'Man's character is his destiny' (Heraclitus). The Greek word for fate is *daimon* - an inner being. Character is our relation to this being - whose silent voice is a questing and destining voice, one that leads us upon our own way of being.

*

Following and Leading - a way and ways

As well as *gathering*, listening also implies 'following' the word of the other and letting it lead one to an understanding of their way of being in the world. Only by following in this way can the listener accompany and 'lead' the other upon their way. Our 'post-modern' world, however, is one in which countless ways of being, ways of thinking and ways of living exist side by side and in competition with one another. This makes following difficult, for each person searches for a way of following their own values and interests, within the maze of competing ways. Some attempt to do this by individualistically refusing to follow others along their way. Others seek sanctuary in the words or beliefs of others, forming communities of 'followers'. Yet following is not a sanctuary in which we stay put. Following means following a way - wherever it might lead us.

One purpose of counselling is to help others to follow their own values, feelings and impulses along whatever way they might lead. We use words to construct signposts along the way. These can also lead us astray. To follow a way is not simply to follow the signposting of language but to explore paths and destinations that are off the track and not yet named by these signposts. To help another person to follow their way means helping them to understand how their existing signposts can literally mis-lead. The crossroads we come to at different stages of our life are often marked by old signposts. To make important life decisions means first questioning the verbal signposts by which we define our alternatives. Change always involves choice or re-choice. But real change is always marked also by a change in the way that we define those choices, by changes in our verbal signposting that are reflected in our language itself.

To follow a different way means to erect new and different signposts for ourselves - instead of clinging to our old language and its signposts whenever we lose our way or come to a crossroads. It means finding a new language by which to regain our bearings. Losing our way - no longer having clear verbal signposts to follow - can be the first step in finding a new language and following a new way. This means taking time to listen to ourselves - for 'leading' requires us to stop at any crossroad and question the value and meaningfulness of the signposts that already mark it. Similarly, following another person as they speak we get a picture of the path which they are following, of the mental rail-tracks and highways marked by their existing vocabulary and the emotional traffic that moves along them. But a listening that leads, that helps another to follow new ways of being rather than rush along pre-established tracks and roadways is a listening that also leads people gently off these tracks and roadways. No listening that merely follows someone's speech, however 'empathically', can help a person to be led by their own being. To be led by our own being means to be led by a listening that hearkens to Being, rather than blindly following the ways of Language. To help another person to be led on their own way of being means helping them to be led by a listening that hearkens to their own being rather than to their existing language. Such a listening - a listening that helps another person to hear and follow themselves is a listening that leads as well as follows.

'From tones at variance comes perfect attunement.'

Heraclitus

A listening that leads is not one that merely attunes empathically to the tones of the speaker's voice, words and feelings but one that also sets a tone at variance with these. This variant tone is not a counter-tone struck by the listener's verbal responses and interpretations but a silent and wordless tone - the fundamental tone of the listener's own being. To follow someone means to be there 'with' them and to stay with them. But we cannot be with someone fully unless we are fully there to ourselves - unless we stay with our own being and its fundamental tone. That is why listening can never be reduced to a set of skills and techniques that we learn in order to listen 'in role' - to listen *as* a counsellor, *as* a teacher, *as* a manager etc. Training in listening 'skills' and 'techniques' implies that it makes no difference *who* is listening as long as the 'how' listening is got right way - conforming to the professional specifications of the role. It presupposes that whilst it makes a difference to a client how 'good' a counsellor is in applying these skills and techniques, it makes no essential difference to the client who the counsellor is, as long as *what* they do and *how* they do it is reasonably 'good'. As a result, the trainee counsellor is not truly called upon to be who they most authentically are - to be themselves with the client and to hearken to the voice of their own being in the listening process.

A counsellor who is not led by their own being - their *daimon* - but instead by trainers and theoretical road maps, is not one who can lead by their listening and can help another person to be led by their own listening. This is a counsellor who is only passively present - present in absence - a 'who' who refrains from fully presencing their own being and instead only listens in role. Presencing one's being, being fully there with the client (*Da-sein* and *Mit-sein*), is confused with being 'directive' in some way. But presencing one's being with others is not the same as re-presenting it in language. Questions about how verbally 'directive' a counsellor, analyst or psychotherapist should be confuse the direction and tone set by their listening. Their words with something quite different - the tone and direction set by their listening as such. The most fundamental misunderstanding of therapeutic listening lies in seeing it only as a necessary means to an end - a mere prelude to finding a more or less meaningful response to a client's speech. It is not recognised that the speech of the client - what they say and the way they say it - is already a response to the inner bearing and embodied presence of the listener - and to the inner direction set by the tone and openness of their listening as such. Neither is it acknowledged that listening is not merely a passive mode of verbal communication but an active form of wordless inner communication through which we can hearken to, presence and communicate the inner voice of our own being. If we are aware that our listening itself is a communication of the inner voice, we can use it to model and embody a way of being and listening that is led by that voice. Therapeutic listening is listening that is intrinsically therapeutic because it is a listening that teaches the client themselves to listen therapeutically to themselves - follow the inner voice of their being rather than being led or mis-lead by their own word and language.

No amount of psychological training in using the 'right' type of words or voice tone in responding to a client can ensure that a listener's verbal and vocal responses are in resonance with the word or *logos* of the *psyche* - and that they resound with and communicate the authentic voice of their own being. Clients immediately sense the depth, tone and openness of a counsellor's listening and are most sensitive to inauthenticity in any shape or form. They themselves hear and perceive what the professional listener is choosing or not choosing to hear and follow - what leads the counsellor. They know intuitively if a counsellor's listening is not led by the inner voice of their own being but merely runs along pre-established professional tracks. They know too if a counsellor's questions are authentic questions that come out of authentic listening or are merely learned and standardised questions through which the counsellor executes their professional role.

In counselling, as in philosophy, there is always the danger that verbally posed questions serve only to maintain and reinforce a learned professional posture. An authentic question on the other hand, whether personal or professional, is one that can bring into view something essentially new - something previously unlearned and *un-heard* of. To bring the hitherto *un-heard* into view however, means first of all to *listen* in a questioning way. This in turn means experiencing listening itself as a way questioning or 'questing', one through which we are able to wordlessly experience the question - to feel and follow it in silence - before framing it in words.

Philosophers seek to name those pre- and trans-personal questions shared and experienced by all human beings. Chief amongst these is the relation of Language and Being. Counsellors on the other hand, focus on personal and inter-personal questions - not questions of Language or Being as such, but the questions raised by particular human beings in a particular language. Yet behind a client's words is their whole 'language of being' - their way of listening to, echoing and translating the wordless call of their own innermost being. The essential focus of 'philosophical counselling', therefore, is not a client's words, body language or silences but their way of responding to the call of their own being - *their way of listening to themselves and others.*

Only by listening to and addressing a client with one's whole being - by silently 'sounding someone out' and not merely echoing or addressing them verbally - are they really 'called', addressed in their very being. What the spoken words of a 'client' essentially reveal or bear forth is not their thoughts or feelings, conscious or 'unconscious', but rather the patience with which they carry or 'bear' themselves pregnantly in silence before speaking - in other words their way of listening to themselves and responding to the call of their own being. To attend to a client's way of listening means listening to the process by which they come to speak - how they come to words or words come to them. We can come to speech impatiently - calling things names with habitual or stereotypical words. Or patiently - letting ourselves be really called and touched by the things we name and choosing with care the words we name them with.

The call that calls to the client is the same call that calls to the counsellor - what Heidegger called 'the call of conscience'. The German word for 'conscience' (*Gewissen*) has a meaning closer to 'knowingness'. The call of conscience is a call that 'comes from me and yet from beyond me'. Heidegger wrote in *Being and Time* of the way in which we 'listen away from' this call - allowing our inner knowing to get overheard and drowned by everyday discourse and 'idle talk'. Idle talk is mere talk 'about' - talk that neither speaks *from* our own being nor truly intends and speaks *to* another being. Idle talk goes against 'the call of conscience' in Heidegger's sense. For 'To let itself get drawn into getting considered and talked about goes against its way of being.'

The call of conscience itself on the other hand 'discourses solely and constantly in the mode of keeping silent.' To overcome our 'listening away' from this call this 'listening away' must itself first of all get 'broken off'.

'In other words the possibility of another kind of hearing...must be given.' To do so the call must first 'find itself as something that has failed to hear itself.'

To be a 'client' is to 'be called' in this way - *to be on the way to finding oneself as someone who has failed to hear oneself.*

Heidegger's exploration of the meaning of 'conscience', 'guilt', and 'care' are all rooted in the idea of the individual becoming aware of their own failure to hear themselves. 'The call' is nothing but the self being silently called to itself and thereby recalled to its 'ownmost potentiality for being'. Only in responding to this call - acknowledging its 'guilt' in failing to hear itself, is this guilt transformed into a committed resolve to *listen* to our innermost being and in doing so become aware of our innermost potentialities of being. This means being present to ourselves and others in a way which resolves to embrace and presence our entire 'being in time' - the whole of our life's journey, including the anxious foreboding of its end. The 'care' that we embody in so doing is not an 'empathic responsiveness' so much as 'response-ability' - a commitment and capacity to listen and hear which is identical with a constant and honest acknowledgement of 'erring' - of not-hearing. This is not an acknowledgement of 'original sin' but a return to an 'original silence'.

The Art of Listening - 'hearing' and 'hearkening'

We do not understand words because we hear them. What we hear is in large part tuned by our pre-understanding of language, people, contexts and situations. Nor does understanding imply that we have really heard. Understanding what has been said is quite different from the ability to hear and recall the words that were spoken - as is shown by the example of foreign language learners.

If we do not understand a foreign language we hear its words as sounds. Even in our own language we hear words as sounds when we have not (yet) understood them as words. As a result we listen. We listen to speech not in order to hear sounds as sounds but to hear them as words - to understand what is being *said* through them. And as soon as we think we understand we stop listening and stop even hearing the words that have been spoken as sounds.

We begin to truly listen when we sense something lacking or questionable in our understanding - a lack that we need to answer by really hearing. Listening, then, is a form of silent and wordless questioning - a 'questing'. But as soon as we think we understand we are no longer questing, no longer listening. That is why active and prolonged listening is rare. Listening is inseparable from a continuous awareness of not fully hearing and not fully understanding. To maintain our listening means maintaining this continuous sense of not-understanding and not-hearing. That is the meaning of 'hearkening'.

Ordinary listening leads to a superficial hearing - one formed by what we already think we understand. Hearkening is a type of listening that leads to a deeper more intensive hearing because it is informed and maintained by a continuous sense of not-hearing and not-understanding. Hearkening is not 'hearing' but 'not-hearing' - not assuming we have already heard all there is to hear in what we hear. To hearken is to be aware of a centre or touchstone of absolute silence within ourselves where we hear nothing. It is by guarding this original silence that we guard our capacity to respond to what calls to us in this silence - not just to respond empathically to others but to hear and caringly awaken the other's 'response-ability' to this call. A response-ability to care for their 'ownmost potentiality for being' (Heidegger).

We hear with the ears. Hearkening means becoming 'all ears', listening with our whole being. We *hear sounds* and audible voice tones but we *hearken to silence* - to the silent tones of feeling that resound within it and to the inner voice that communicates through it. Hearkening is not just a listening receptivity to this voice, however. It is also a way of communicating from it - an 'inner voice communication'. Martin Buber emphasised that it is only in genuinely attuning to and making contact with the inner self of another human being - a 'you'- that we enter a true relation with our own inner being - the eternal 'You'. By itself our inner self is no-self. Its voice is voiceless, except when it speaks to someone and knows whom it is speaking to. We can never 'express' our inner being except by intending and addressing someone from it - intending this 'you' and no other. By intending this person and no other with our listening we can also intend or 'mean' it to convey a specific meaning or intent - to bear back a message. In sounding out another person with our own essential tone of being we embody and presence our inner being. In this way we also reach out to and contact the inner being of the client. We set up a carrier wave of inner communication on which we both receive and transmit messages through our listening. We not only attune 'empathically' to the multiple voices that we hear in the client's speech and which each of us bear within us. We attune also to an inner voice that belongs to no-one in particular and yet to all, which is neither 'mine' nor 'yours', 'his' nor 'hers', 'ours' nor 'theirs'. This is not the voice of the linguistic 'I' or ego. It is the self experienced as another - not as an 'I' but as a 'you'.

The Listening Body - 'holding' and 'handling'

In a quite tangible way we can 'hold' someone in our gaze. In a similar way we can hold someone in our listening attention - in our 'aural gaze'. We become aware of someone holding us in their listening gaze when we feel it subtly deepening the way we listen to ourselves as we speak. 'Handling' is the silent modulation of the tone and touch of our listening gaze, turning it into a carrier wave on which messages are transmitted as well as received.

When we sound people out with our feelings we are also feeling them - touching what I call their listening body. The felt sense we have of someone as they talk to us is not just passive. As we hear them out, our own response begins to gather. As well as being touched, we begin to actively respond to this touch by gently and quietly feeling around. We are feeling with our 'listening body'. And what this feels as it feels around is the listening body of the other. The other person's words are the outer surface or skin of this body, its verbal sheath. Beneath, we can register the sensitivity of their listening body, sensing in advance how they will respond to the words and tone of voice which we think of adopting and the degree to which they will feel inwardly touched by our response.

To talk of 'touch' here is not a 'mere' metaphor. Listening is itself a form of 'inner vibrational touch' (Seth). As listeners we touch each other with the tendrils of our intent - the fibres of our listening body. And yet it is an intrinsic part of many cultures (not least English culture) that such intimate inner touch should be 'politely' avoided in communication. As a result, people rely solely on probing each other with their words and therefore must do so as sensitively and politely as they can. Handling people by 'sensitively' adjusting our language and tone of voice compensates to a certain degree for handling them through the silent tone and touch of our listening. The alternative - to become mutually conscious of the inner touch involved in listening is threateningly close to the type of intimacy of relating that is associated with close relationships and physical touch. Inner touch is therefore restricted to the therapist's consulting room, in the same way that sex is restricted to the bedroom. This reflects a general social taboo on silence and inner touch, inner 'holding' and 'handling'. It is this taboo that makes language and verbal communications into totems - charged with symbolic and sexual significance.

One context in which physical touch is permitted outside of sex, albeit with reservations or spurious innuendo - is through therapeutic massage. If massage is to be sensitive and healing it must be more than just a set of mechanical skills or techniques. It must be grounded in the physical attunement of the practitioner, and embody this attunement through a responsive 'listening' to muscle tone and a sensitive handling of energy. Similarly, if listening is to be therapeutic it must transcend the intellectual or 'analytic' framework of the listener as well as their immediate emotional reactions. It must be grounded in attunement to feeling tone, and in the listener's capacity to sense and resonate, touch and respond to others through the medium of feeling tone.

The word 'analysis' derives from the Greek *analuein* - to loosen or free up. Therapeutic listening and therapeutic massage are both 'analysis' in this essential sense. Therapeutic massage is an art of physical communication or 'messaging' through bodily touch, holding and handling. Its medium is the living tissue of the physical body. The massage practitioner probes gently beneath its skin and loosens the meaningful currents of energy that circulate within tissue. That is perhaps why the Greek word for 'touch' means also 'to kindle'. Therapeutic listening is itself a form of psychic 'massage' - a form of inner holding and inner handling - a kindling. The listener probes gently beneath the linguistic surface or skin of the listening body to loosen and free the energetic currents of meaning that circulate within and beneath words. The listening body is like a plant. Its roots grow down into the smallest cavities of our inwardly felt body. They infiltrate the inner spaces of our thoughts, and of our very cells. The listening body can send out subtle tendrils of intent that touch the other inwardly. And when we truly listen, it opens leaves that breathe in and absorb the embodied presence of the other, drawing out their inner light and warmth of soul.

The Discipline of Listening - 'heeding' and 'withholding'

'Although this *logos* holds forever, men fail to comprehend it, both before hearing it and after they have heard.'

Heraclitus

Listening is not something we do in between stretches of speech. It is what we do in order to hearken to the silence that precedes speech, to *heed* someone's words *after* they have been spoken and to allow our own response to gather wordlessly *before* we respond.

'Man is encased in an armour whose task it is to ward off signs.' (Buber). The fact that we have heard a person out does not mean that we have taken their words in - heeded their unspoken message. To do so we need to delay immediate verbal response and allow a continuing period of silence after we have heard someone out. The more quickly and impatiently we respond to another person's words, the less time we give ourselves to really heed them. It is taken for granted in all discussions of counselling skills, that listening involves hearing someone out and not interrupting or foreclosing their speech. If we feel an urge to respond as soon as possible it is difficult to know if we have really heard someone out. Perhaps the person we are listening to has indeed finished speaking - has spoken out all that they wish to say for the time being. This does not mean that we have heard them out. For there is a difference between hearing a person out and hearing their words out. 'Hearing out' means not only hearing out the person and letting them finish. It also means giving ourselves and the speaker time to heed the words that have already been spoken - to let *them* speak to us and reverberate within us.

How long either the counsellor or client talks at any one time - the length of their conversational 'turn' - is not as important as the interval of silence between these turns. It is in this turn interval that the words that have already been spoken can linger in the air and reverberate within us. If we allow them to do so, we hear language speaking - we hear a client's words as the echo of a silent communication of being - the voice of 'the between'.

The depth of both philosophical dialogue and the counselling conversation are related to the length of the turn interval and to the depth of silence it facilitates. For no matter how short or long people's turns, ordinary conversational patterns, at least in Western culture, reduce the interval of silence *between* turns to an absolute minimum - most often to zero or less than zero. Instead, the turning point of conversation, the point at which the listener begins to speak and the speaker to listen, occurs shortly after - or even before - the speaker has finished speaking. The turning point of our listening, on the other hand, is the point at which our inner listening response to a speaker begins to transform itself into an outward verbal response. If the interval of silence between listening and speaking is minimised, this turning occurs while someone is speaking and therefore before we have given time for their words to resonate within us.

Philosophical counselling demands a fundamental alteration in the timing of our response - re-situating the central turning point of our listening to a point after someone has finished uttering their words. This grants time to take in what has been said and to heed the words that have been used to say it. Only by withholding our verbal and vocal response in this way do we learn to stay in contact and communication with others without speaking - to trust that our own inner response will communicate wordlessly.

The minimalisation of the turn interval in Western culture, not only in everyday conversation but also in philosophical and counselling dialogue, forecloses our listening. It prevents us from experiencing the questing that arises in the gap between language and being. If our thoughts and emotions sometimes reduce us to silence and wordlessness, this silence and wordlessness is not so much 'resistance' to them as an opportunity to listen to ourselves in a new way. It encourages us to find new modes of discourse which not only tolerate but encourage and demand proper periods of silence and wordlessness - time for listening, time for attending to language, time to be and to communicate our being. Time to allow what is gathering within us to speak to us - to 'listen to the logos'. To counsel means to grant time for listening in this way.

The protocol of withholding does not imply that the longer the turn interval the deeper the dialogue. For, the physical time that elapses between hearing someone out and giving a response is less important than the psychological time-space that expands within this physical time interval. The physical time interval allows an inward expansion of psychological time - of 'meaning space'. When we give ourselves time to read a book or listen to a piece of music meditatively we also experience an inward expansion of psychological time and allow the meaning space 'between the lines' or 'between the notes' to open up. We open ourselves to the interplay of the outer word and the inner word, the *logos prophorikos* and the *logos endiathetos* - the said and the unsaid.

The unsaid is a common pool of unasked and unanswered questions to which both listener and speaker, both counsellor and client respond in their thoughts and feelings, their words and gestures. If a counsellor, therapist or analyst 'thinks' something but does not say it, he or she need not be surprised if a client 'picks it up' and articulates it - or vice versa. It has not simply been '*un*-said' but un-*said* - left on the table of silence for the other person to pick up. Perhaps not naming or describing it in our terms, but in their own. In not expressing a thought aloud, the latter does not disappear, nor is it telepathically transmitted verbatim. It communicates through the silent tone of our listening.

Listening always involves 'unsaying' - leaving things unsaid. Speaking is a response to the unsaid. Language the tool with which we name it. To hint at the unsaid in implicit language is like pointing to what is there between us on this table or altar of silence. Describing it in language that is too explicit can be like picking an object up from this table - or even wresting it out of the other person's hands - and brandishing it. Language that is merely explicit leaves the table emptied, the silence bare. Meaning then evaporates. Conversely, to leave something unsaid - to 'withhold' a particular thought, feeling, or interpretation - can mean that I let it rest in the silence between us, or that I cover and conceal it in words. Yet there is a third way of withholding - a genuine 'with-holding'. This means holding the object on the table with the other person, hand on hand - helping them to feel safe in handling it by handling it with them.

Silence can be threatening because the objects on the altar of silence are threatening, because I fear to look at them, hold or handle them psychically. It can also be threatening because I wish to hide them in silence, fearing they may otherwise be mis-interpreted, lost to me or substituted with other objects. I can fear so much that I allow nothing to appear on the table, try to wipe it clear or cover it with a verbal tablecloth. The silence that opens up when a counsellor withholds immediate response and allows an interval of silence can be threatening because it exposes this table. It is made safe by with-holding - by holding and handling its objects together. What are these objects? They are not things, nor even thoughts and feelings. They are our silent and unstated questions. Withholding means *holding* these unstated questions *with* the other, questing with them rather than answering their questions for them or posing questions to them. It does not mean that we withdraw aloofly into ourselves. What we hold back is only a premature outward response - verbal or physical. This gives us a chance to heed the inner resonance of a person's words and hearken to the silent questing of their being.

Withholding and silent, listening attunement automatically sets a tone 'at variance' with the client's own way of listening and responding. That is because interplay of client and counsellor is a dialogue between contrasting tonalities or wavelengths of attunement as well as between contrasting approaches to the *timing* of the 'turn intervals' between address and response. The client may be unsettled by the silence occasioned by the counsellor's withholding of immediate responses, and continue to respond themselves without any interval of silence whenever the counsellor has spoken. In such a case the counsellor cannot immediately seek to slow the tempo of dialogical exchange, but must gradually introduce longer pauses and periods of withholding. The manner of doing so also embodies the counsellor's handling of the client and of the questions they raise.

The protocol of withholding carries the same significance in philosophical counselling as the basic rule of so-called 'free association' in psychoanalysis - that the analysand should speak whatever comes into their minds. Withholding is in a certain sense a contrary principle, suggesting that we should give time for impressions to gather force within us (*legein*) before translating these impressions into words or images. It applies in the first place to counsellors themselves, providing them not only with the time-space necessary to really heed a client's words, but with a parameter by which to gauge the quality and patience of the client's own listening - their capacity to with-hold and heed.

In psychoanalysis, silence on the part of the client may be interpreted as a form of resistance. In philosophical counselling the only 'resistance' is resistance to silence - to allowing ourselves to 'pause for thought' and listen inwardly. Personality is the way we bear ourselves forth in speech. Character is the way we *bear ourselves in silence*. The focus of philosophical counselling is the character of a client's listening, the *inner bearing* of their silence. This is reflected in body language. The more uncomfortable we are with silence, the more this shows itself in our posture. The discomfort expresses an incapacity to *be* and to *embody* our being in silence. We cannot really be with others in silence unless we can 'bear' ourselves in this silence. This means finding an inner bearing and posture through which we can both stay in contact with our selves and be with others. In speech we often engage in contact with others whilst at the same time losing contact with ourselves. In listening we often do the reverse. Withholding provides an opportunity to learn how to be in silence - to find our bearings psychically and physically. Our body language in silence reveals the tension between psychically withdrawing and physically presencing ourselves, being with ourselves and being with others, listening inwardly and listening outwardly.

To listen means to 'list' or lean. When we listen we lean inwardly towards another with our whole being. The listing of the listener cannot be reduced to 'body language'. To 'lean towards another with an open posture' as instructed by manuals on listening and body language is no guarantee that we are really listening - merely that we are giving the physical appearance of listening. It is our inner bearing and comportment as listeners that is the basis of our intellectual position, our emotional stance and our physical posture itself. An inner bearing is our inner relation to both being and language, manifest in the way we hearken and heed. The essential inner bearing of the philosophical counsellor - that of withholding - is not a repressive or constrictive holding back and keeping silent but the bearing that first frees and clears a space for deep listening.

'We understand only too well that a thinker would prefer to hold back the word that is to be said, not in order to keep it for himself, but to bear it towards the encounter with what is to be thought.'

Martin Heidegger

Withholding does not imply that we abandon the quest for words that can name and describe those wordless felt comprehensions that gather within us as we listen. It is itself a wordless listening quest for the naming word, one which gives expression to a paradox which Heidegger recognised as the central question of language itself: 'How is he to give a name to what he is still questing for? To assign the naming word is after all, what constitutes finding.'

The Protocols of Philosophical Group Counselling
- The 'Listening Circle'

In the context of group therapy the principle of **withholding** can be formalised in what I call a 'listening circle'. Two basic ground rules or protocols are necessary to establish a listening circle. These are also the basic protocols of philosophical counselling, providing a framework of interaction that encourages a listening dialogue.

Protocol 1
The first protocol is that no participant in the group shall respond immediately to another, but shall instead allow a variable period of silence - a 'turn interval' in which to **heed** and **hearken**.

Protocol 2
The second protocol is that no participant shall address their questions or statements directly to another member of the group. This protocol helps people

(a)   to communicate by **hinting** - to intend a message for another person inwardly, indirectly and implicitly rather than outwardly, directly and explicitly,

(b)   to **heed** their own questions - questions they would usually pass on by addressing them to another member of the group and challenging that person to answer for them.

By **withholding** from direct questioning they open themselves instead to receive an answering call from their own being - or from the group. For as each person's words linger in silence, others can also heed them - hear them as responses to their own wordless or unspoken questions, as bearers of a message from themselves.

Many counsellors are trained to communicate through explicit statements and questions. Communication that is entirely explicit, however, says nothing. Conversely, what is left implicit or un-said in communication is what most essentially communicates in all communication, as it does in poetry. Leaving something un-said is not merely a 'not-saying'. It says something. *Un*-saying is also un-*saying.*

An entirely explicit statement conceals the inner questing of our being and carries no questioning undertone. By **hearkening** to and **heeding** the deeper unspoken questions that are only *hinted at* by a person's words (including their own) participants can also learn to use language in a more sensitive and conscious way - to hint. **Hinting** means using language to communicate implicit meanings, messages and questions that cannot be fully explicated *in* words but only communicated *through* the word (*dia-logos*). It is the task of the philosophical counsellor to model the language of **hinting**, to transform the word into a bearer of an inner message, an act of unsaying. This is in one sense a paradoxical strategy, for as Heidegger noted: 'To hear a hint, one must first...hear oneself into the region from which it comes.' It is by the practice of **withholding** that this region also opens itself to our hearing, often in a quite striking and dramatic way. Experiencing an extended silence in the turn-interval people begin to hear *under* language. After taking part in a listening circle they begin to recognise in retrospect the superficiality of discussions characterised by rapid verbal exchange in which the pregnancy of silence is aborted or miscarried in speech.

The listening circle is the 'experiential' basis of education in philosophical counselling. Its 'theoretical' basis is a philosophy of listening and of counselling. Experiential and theoretical education are not separated but interwoven both theoretically and experientially. All philosophical dialogue concerning 'theoretical' issues becomes 'experiential' when it is conducted under the protocols of the listening circle. These can also be formalised in a one-to-one setting - treating it as a group of two, and transforming discussion into a listening dialogue. Through a listening dialogue one-to-one tutoring in philosophy ceases to be merely academic or theoretical and becomes a form of 'mentoring' - philosophy as counselling and counselling as philosophy. The tutor responds to the student neither as an academic philosopher nor as a personal counsellor but as a philosophical counsellor and mentor - modelling and embodying a new way of listening.

The basic stance of the philosophical counsellor acknowledges that all questions are fundamentally shared questions, questions that arise in the ever-present gap between language and being. This stance can only be maintained if it is reflected in a different way of speaking - a speaking grounded in listening. Whenever a philosophical counsellor listens to people speak *about* something, he or she must be aware of what they are saying *to* each other, *to* the group, or *to* the counsellor through their words. This does not imply that the counsellor should interpret implicit meanings in words, like an individual or group analyst. The point is not to interpret implicit meanings in words (to make them explicit) but to receive and respond to them on the same level - wordlessly and implicitly. The counsellor must be aware of language as the metaphor of an ongoing and silent dialogue of being - and participate in this dialogue. This means two things: responding silently from their own being to the language of the other, and responding with their own language (and not through learned or borrowed ways of speaking) to the being of the other.

To be a philosopher is to think. This means to be a listener. To be a listener means being able to fully *be* in silence with another. Not to depend on language and speech in order to actively presence one's own being. The 'authority' of the counsellor is the authenticity of their own *language of being* and their own listening responsiveness to the client's language of being. The vocation of the counsellor is to *be* (in) *listening* - thereby to **hearken** to what calls to us from another human being. This is not so much a role as an inner vocation shared by all - for to have a vocation is to respond to a calling.

Philosophical counselling is not linked to particular professional or theoretical languages. Its 'theoretical' focus is the nature of language and being. Its 'practical' focus is the client's characteristic way of listening to and translating their own language of being. The way we word our own experience reflects our listening self-consciousness of language - our capacity to speak our own being and to discriminate between its voice and the voices of language. At the same time 'wording is worlding'. Our way of 'being in the world' embodies our way of 'being in the word' - of dwelling in the meaning space housed by language. This meaning space is more than just the semantics of words. It includes the meaningful psychic interiority of our own bodies and the meaningful psychic exteriority of the bodies around us - the people, objects and events of our world.

The proliferating schools of psychoanalysis, counselling and therapy each compete to assert the universality and truth of their own theoretical languages. Philosophy grounds our understanding of all these languages in the native language of the psyche - the language of inner tonality or resonance. Philosophical listening is meditative listening - a deeper way of hearing and under-standing the vocabularies employed by both clients and professional helpers themselves. The point is not to rely on any theoretical perspectives as a touchstone for our listening but to find an inner touchstone - the inner voice. And yet to develop an adequate philosophy of listening means also finding a language by which to describe the inner activity of listening.

Hearkening, holding, handling, heeding, withholding and **hinting** are some of the basic elements of this language of listening, its philosophical and experiential keywords. Learning to counsel philosophically does not mean learning a theory but learning to experience what these keywords mean in practice. Education in philosophical counselling involves introducing the keywords to others in a thoughtful and living way. This is achieved not through writing, speaking or intellectual discussion alone - through talking about the keywords, but through a mode of discourse which at the same time embodies them - listening dialogue and listening circles. For we cannot discuss the subject of listening deeply unless we are at the same time listening and seeking to deepen that listening.

A listening dialogue cannot be reduced to verbal communication, non-verbal body language, emotional expression or intellectual discussion. 'Talking about' and 'expressing' are aspects of communication. A listening dialogue is a **hearkening** to the intercourse of being that underlies verbal communication. From this **hearkening** it seeks to name what it is that the verbal communication itself is essentially 'about'. In 'On the Way to Language' Heidegger presents 'A Dialogue on Language' with a Japanese interlocutor. In the course of this dialogue he mentions his conversations with a certain Count Kuki:

> 'Our dialogues were not formal, scholarly discussions. Whenever that sort of thing seemed to be taking place, Count Kuki remained silent...They made the Eastasian world more luminously present, and the dangers of our dialogues became more clearly visible.'

The danger in question was that of trying to talk about Eastasian art and poetry in European terms, and that in this process: **'the language of the dialogue constantly destroyed the possibility of saying what**

the dialogue was about.' This is a danger that attends all counselling and therapeutic conversations. And yet it is our very awareness of it that can transform such conversation into a listening dialogue.

Going on Being - Heidegger and Winnicott

In his essay 'On Communication' Winnicott wrote of the healthy use of 'active non-communication' for the purpose of 'feeling real', as opposed to communication that expresses the compliant behaviour of a 'false self'. Notably, he describes this false self as born of an early interference in just 'going on being'.

Compliance can be expressed in the very act of speaking, irrespective of content, which may be a denial of our freedom to dwell silently within the reality of our own being and hearken to its tones. Compliance can also manifest itself in speech as role compliance - using the 'right' words and phrases, the 'right' register or emotional vocabulary. Equally, compliance may govern our way of listening - adopting the 'right' tone of voice and body posture, asking the 'right' sort of questions. Then we are no longer listening with our whole being, but listening in role - listening as a counsellor, as an analyst, as a parent, friend or helper.

Uniquely amongst psychoanalytic thinkers, Winnicott, like Heidegger, used a language that spoke of being. 'After being, doing and being done to. But first, being.' He spoke of the mother's 'holding' of the infant as 'keeping the baby safe from unpredictable and therefore traumatic events that interrupt going-on-being'. Going-on-being is contrasted with environmental unreliability, the need to react to external 'impingements' and the threat of annihilation:

'In this place which is characterised by the essential existence of a holding environment, the 'inherited potential' (of the infant) is becoming a 'continuity of being'. The alternative to being is reacting, and reacting interrupts being and annihilates. Being and annihilation are the two alternatives. The holding environment therefore has as its main function the reduction to a minimum of impingements to which the infant must react with resultant annihilation of personal being.'

Winnicott also speaks of the mother's 'handling' of the infant: 'Handling describes the environmental provision that corresponds roughly with the establishment of a psycho-somatic partnership'. Through her careful handling of the infant's body, the infant's psyche feels able to dwell safely within its body. Winnicott emphasises the importance of this 'indwelling' to the infant's sense of 'going-on-being'.

The word infant derives from the Latin *in-fans*: not-speaking. As we acquire language we learn to handle and protect ourselves with words. The mother tongue replaces the mother. But the transition to verbal communication often goes hand in hand, not only with the gradual separation of mother and child, but with a growing rift between language and being. Winnicott described this rift as the splitting off of an intellectual 'false self' from the psyche-soma. The latter remains the location of a 'true self', but one that has now become an incommunicable core.

Winnicott implies that psychopathology is in some way a result of failures in environmental provision - of adequate holding and handling. Heidegger, on the other hand, saw the schizoid rift between language and being not as the exceptional result of personal upbringing, but as the ruling framework of our technical-industrial world. Such is the rift between language and being that characterises the media-, market- and technology-driven society that the therapeutic listening demanded by so-called 'depressive', 'schizophrenic' or 'borderline' individuals is not simply a response to an individual pathology but to a social one. Mental illness challenges us to acknowledge the absence or foreclosure of real listening in social life. To remedy this absence we can only start with ourselves, by removing the barriers that prevent us from really listening with our whole being.

'There are many, many people living in private dungeons today, people who give no evidence of it whatever on the outside, where you have to listen very sharply to hear the faint message from the dungeon.' Rogers

Winnicott saw a reparative role for psychoanalysis. Heidegger saw a reparative role for philosophy in restoring the link between language and being. Whereas for Winnicott, as for Freud, psychoanalysis was a 'talking cure', for Heidegger philosophical thinking was a 'listening cure' - linked in its very essence to the way we hear language, hear each other and respond to the call of our own being. Those trapped in the dungeon are not simply not heard, they are also not listening. The way we were listened to as infants and children has no doubt a great influence on our capacity to listen to ourselves. But no matter how little we were heard in our early years, one way that we can overcome the psychological deformations or disturbances that may have resulted is by learning to listen to others. Perhaps this is one of the things that lead people to want to train as counsellors. Perhaps also one of the key desires of the client in counselling is not simply to be heard, but to learn to listen and hear. It is through learning to listen to others that we learn to hear ourselves just as it is through learning to hear ourselves that we learn to listen to others.

Significantly, Winnicott speaks of the analyst **holding** the patient by 'conveying *in words* [my stress] at the appropriate moment something that shows that the analyst knows and understands the deepest anxiety that is being experienced or that is waiting to be experienced.' And yet just as the mother's way of physically holding and handling the infant depends on her sensitivity to the infant, so the way we handle ourselves and others in speech depends on how we come to words or they to us - depends on the way we listen.

The importance of a philosophy and psychology of listening is constantly obscured by the false controversy over whether mental illness is 'caused' by environmental or genetic factors, a debate which conceals the true genealogy of character. 'Genealogy' implies speaking about the way things come to be - their genesis. The way we speak about how things come to be affects the way they come to be. The genealogy of character is the way we each come to be who we are through the word (*dia-logos*). This depends both on our acquired language and the thought patterns these embody, and on the way we listen. Our way of listening determines how we 'think' - how we choose words and how we hear and respond to them. This also affects how we respond to our genetic inheritance.

Proponents of genetic 'causality' may admit that environmental factors influence whether particular genes will manifest in physical or mental illness, just as proponents of environmental causality may admit that genetic factors may affect our response to environmental impingements. Yet whilst both geneticists and environmentalists use their own biological, sociological or psychological languages to explain psychopathology it is paradoxical that neither acknowledges the role of language as such in the life of the individual and society. Language shapes the way we interpret and respond to both our own genetic inheritance and to our environmental or social inheritance. The task of philosophy is to remind us that we cannot explain things in scientific, psychiatric or psychoanalytic terms unless we question what it is that we are seeking to explain with it. To talk, for example about the 'causes' of 'schizophrenia' or 'depression' assumes that we know what it is that these terms name. To say that they 'categorise groups of symptoms' does not mean that they are based on empirical facts - for symptoms themselves are described and interpreted in words. We forget that both words were coined within the last two centuries. Are we to assume that because a word such as 'depression' has a contemporary or 'scientific' ring it is better than older ones such as 'melancholy'?

The genealogy of mental illness has as much do with the way in which society comes to use terms such as 'stress' and 'depression' as it does with the way in which individuals come to handle and shape their self-experience in words. The individual and social dimensions of wording are intimately connected. For it is when the language of everyday discourse fails the individual that he or she takes recourse to forms of speech and communication that appear 'pathological'. This is mirrored in the way society itself takes recourse to the language of pathology - to medical, psychiatric and psychoanalytic terminologies. Such institutionalised modes of discourse often bear within them the same 'schizoid', or 'paranoid' pathology that confronts society in the patient. The language of 'psychopathology' in other words, to some degree embodies the very pathologies it describes. A classic example is the writings of Melanie Klein, imbued as they are with their own clearly paranoid language and tone.

For Heidegger the essence of all 'pathology' was *forgetfulness of being*. This is mirrored in a forgetfulness of language and its history. Heidegger used etymology to challenge this linguistic amnesia - to remind us, for example, that the word 'logic' derives from the Greek *logos*. If we listen to the word 'genealogy' in a similar way we can hear it speaking not about the genesis of things but about the genesis of speech and of the word - *logos*. The word 'Genealogy' also says 'logogenesis'. 'Genealogy' - the way we come to be, and 'logogenesis' - the way the word comes to be are one. We come to *be* who we are through the word and we come to the *word* from who we are. The way we listen is the way we come to ourselves through the word and come to the word from within ourselves.

Listening also re-links the inner speech or *logos* of the *psyche* with what Winnicott called the *psyche-soma* - with our felt bodily sense of meaning. This is composed of those wavelengths of attunement that constitute 'feeling tone'. They are the inner resonance or logos of the psyche. They are also its pathos - the basis of 'empathy' and 'telepathy' as well as of 'pathology'. A philosophical understanding of 'pathology' rooted in etymology pays heed to *logogenesis* (the coming to be of the word) and *etymo-logos* (the truth of the word) in a quite different way to either psychoanalysis or academic philology. A philosophical psychiatry would need to pay heed to the nature of listening in a deeper way than psychotherapy and counselling, understanding it - as Freud himself did - as a medium of silent 'telepathic' as well as 'empathic' communication. Winnicott himself distinguished between what he called explicit and indirect communication - including verbal communication - and something that he termed 'silent communication'. He saw the latter as an attempt to restore a sense of reality - of being one's real self - and yet he denied its inter-personal reality, regarding it as a communication with personal and 'subjective objects' only.

'Here communication is not non-verbal; it is, like the music of the spheres, absolutely personal. It belongs to being alive...The two extremes, explicit communication that is indirect, and silent or personal communication that feels real, each of these has its place, and in the intermediate cultural area there exists for many, but not for all, a mode of communication which is a most valuable compromise.'

The analogy with 'the music of the spheres' is a telling one. When we listen to someone speak there is a sense in which we hear them play their own music. Their words are not their music but an interpretation of it - like lyrics put to a melody. Their voices are not their music but their way of singing these lyrics. Their body language is not their music, but their way of playing this music - of embodying it. The images that this music generates in us *are not* the music. They are our way of 'dreaming' that music. Music is not reducible to mental images, notes on a score or even actual sounds. We hear music not as sounds but *through* those sounds. We do so through inner resonance with 'sounds of silence' - those silent feeling tone that *re-sound* in the 'sound of music' and are the very source of musical composition. In a similar way we can hear the inner music of another human being- the music of feeling tone that re-sounds in their speech and in their silence. And we can respond to that music not only with words but with the music of our own feeling tones - embodied and emanated through the instrument or *organon* of our own organism.

According to Bollas the infant is in thrall to the mother's 'performance'. And yet the way she handles the infant is not her music but her playing of this music. This playing can be mechanical and erratic or sensitively attuned - musical. If it is musical then it is based not simply on a listening receptivity to her own being, but on a sensitive attunement to the 'music' of the infant - to the unique tone colours that make up its essential language of being. Then the music that is played is not hers alone but a common music. In quite general terms, any genuinely *listening* relation of self and other, like that of infant and mother, can be compared to that of musicians performing a duet. Each musician plays their own music in listening sensitivity and resonance with the music of the other. The audible tones they produce through their playing are not the music as such but are an artful bodying of the essential music of feeling tone. The music they each body in their playing is in this sense not 'theirs' at all, but rather their way of hearing and responding to the inner call of this music. A call that each knows as something that 'comes from me and yet from beyond me' (Martin Heidegger).

CHARGING THE QUESTION

Questioning in the Counselling Dialogue

The purpose of this essay is to introduce a new philosophical understanding of listening in the counselling or therapeutic relationship. This understanding challenges the typical interrogative framework of the counselling dialogue based principally on the use of elicitative questions and directed towards the verbal representation and clarification of a client's 'issues'. The way of listening I call 'maieutic' on the other hand, involves a discipline of sustained withholding of verbal questioning and elicitation, and instead emphasises the importance of authentically *dialogical* response - one that speaks both in silence and 'through' the word (*dia-logos*).

In ordinary social communication, lack of outward responsiveness is usually taken as a sign of indifference or unresponsiveness. But the fact that we do not immediately react outwardly to what someone says does not mean that we are inwardly unreceptive and unresponsive. True inner responsiveness depends on our capacity not to react immediately when someone has finished speaking, but instead to allow a period of silence in which to take in what has been said and give it a 'second hearing' within oneself - to listen to ourselves before responding and in this way give ourselves time to heed and tune our inner responses.

People often speak in order to avoid listening to themselves and others, giving their own inner responses to others no time to mature but overriding and foreclosing them with automatic or 'pat' reactions. For giving time to heed ourselves inwardly and respond to others from a deeper place might require 'awkward' intervals of silence before speaking. Unfortunately this taboo on silence and on truly meditative and thoughtful listening and response affects professional counsellors and therapists as much as it does people untrained in 'helping' skills. Counselling and therapy are themselves identified with offering helpful forms of outward response to others, not in the form of interruptions, unconsidered reactions or 'know it all' advice but in the form of sensitive exploratory questions, validating acknowledgement or 'mirroring'' reformulations of what the other person has said. Pick up almost any transcript of a counselling session and a typical structure reveals itself, for the counsellor's responses almost invariably take the principal form either of questions or of echoing statements uttered in a questioning tone. The interrogative structure of the counselling dialogue has deep roots in Western culture, going back to the question-and-answer pattern exemplified in the Socratic dialogues recorded by Plato. Socrates responds to his interlocutors with thoughtful, pertinent and challenging verbal questions, aiming to elicit through these questions a truer understanding of the matter being discussed. But there is a danger and grave limitation to this model of dialogue, and the style of counselling which embodies it. The danger is that 'understanding' is identified only with our ability to represent a matter or answer a question clearly in words. Getting to the 'truth' means finding words, which represent a matter or answer a question accurately.

Why is this a danger? The term dialogue comes from the Greek *dia-logos* - 'through the word'. But what communicates through people's words can never be fully represented or defined in words. Nor can words - even those of a counsellor - ever be used 'neutrally', merely to echo, reflect or represent something without judgement or bias. For something invariably communicates through our verbal responses to others - even if they take the form of open questions and tentative enquiries - that is not represented *in* them. The danger is that what communicates through the word is disguised and concealed in the word - by the very matters that it represents. Responding to a client with verbal questions, however 'sensitively' put and appropriate, can easily become a way of fending off the inner questions raised in the counsellor by a client's words - a way of not having to feel these questions and of not having to respond to them inwardly as well as in words.

'A question that is not really *my* question, that is not a charged question for me, creates an uneasy tension in the client, implying a relationship between two things that the other person hasn't yet made.' Karin Heinitz

And in seeking to respond to a counsellor's questions, it becomes very difficult for a client to hear the hidden implications of these questions - the theoretical and experiential assumptions that communicate through them. Having been asked a question the client immediately turns inward to seek an answer, rather than giving themselves time to first hear through the question to what it implies about the counsellor's own stance - to the message it conveys.

It is a core element of Western thinking to put questions in words, to evaluate the 'truth' of the words used to answer these questions, whilst at the same time ignoring the presuppositions of the questions themselves and the words used to put them. Yet in the last analysis, just as there are no statements that people can make which are absolute truth and which do not conceal hidden questions, so there are also no questions people can ask which do not conceal hidden statements. Counselling as well as philosophy can easily degenerate into a form of Socratic, question-and-statement type 'dialogue' which denies and disguises this basic truth. For in seeking to hear the questions implied by or communicated through another person's statements, we easily *overhear* the implicit statements we make through our own questions.

I believe that the central challenge of both philosophy and counselling, if they are not to degenerate into intellectual or emotional 'language games', is to be really open to those essential life questions shared by all human beings. For a counsellor to be really open to a client's life questions - whether articulated or merely implied - means more than just being able to represent, explore and refine a question in words. It means being able to *experience* the question and to affirm it *as* a question. These two go together. To experience a question means experiencing it wordlessly. Only by allowing ourselves to experience a question wordlessly do we experience it as an authentic question - an open question. For every verbal formulation of a question to some extent predisposes a certain type of answer and therefore forecloses the question as a question. It may be hard for the reader to understand what I mean by 'experiencing a question wordlessly'. Yet this is exactly what it means to listen. Listening is a way of *questing* understanding, not by putting questions in words but by holding open the gap between what another person represents to us in their words and what communicates through them - 'what they mean to us'. 'What they mean to us' has two intonations - what the other person seeks to say to us through their words (what *they* mean to us) and what their words themselves say to us (what they mean *to us*). The *relation* between these two dimensions of meaning is itself a question for both listener and speaker, counsellor and client - one that underlies all other questions. Though it is a dynamic relation it cannot be reduced to any theoretically described dynamic such as 'transference' or 'counter-transference'. Psychodynamic theories posit all sorts of possible 'transferential' connections between an individual's past and present experience, and between their experience and that of the counsellor or psychotherapist. This is itself dangerous, because it leads the listener to make theoretical connections and present these as hypotheses to be confirmed or denied by the client - to see hypothetical connections and then try and get the speaker to 'fill them in'. A genuine question on the other hand - a question that has real charge for the listener, is not a hypothetical positive relation. It is an experienced absence of relationship - an absence of relationship between two things, one which may at the same time express an absent relation between two people.

Where a relationship is unclear or missing, questions become a way of articulating an absence or obscurity of connection. A verbal question - any question - is essentially a way of representing this absent relation, this missing connection between two things and two people. The problem is that every way of posing a question in words, of representing the absent relation, itself implies a certain type of answer or positive relation. In addition it places a demand on the client to 'make' some sort of mental or emotional connection of the sort implied by the counsellor's question without first experiencing the very absence of relation that the question represents. A counsellor can help a client to do this only by doing it themselves - by allowing themselves to fully experience the absent relation inwardly. This gives the relation charge, rather like an electrical charge or polarity building up between two metal plates or two clouds. If a question is allowed to experientially charge itself in this way, connections do not need to be 'made'. At a certain point in the build up of charge the connection sparks - the experience of genuine insight. The difference between insight and artificially 'made' connections is like the difference between charging two plates and letting them spark and simply sticking a wire between them to convey the charge. Too often counsellors offer their clients wires to connect the plates without first letting them build up any charge. When no current flows (essentially because the question itself is a dead or chargeless one) the client is then accused of resistance or 'attacks on linking'. At the same time they feel pressured to invent a meaningful answer for the counsellor - to simulate a flow of energy.

In electrodynamic terminology, the process of allowing a charge to build up and then discharge is called 'capacitance'. The capacity of the listener to experience a question inwardly and let it build up charge is also a sort of energetic capacitance. Only unspoken questions gather charge in this way. Every charged question acknowledges an absent relation, not only between two things but also between the client and the counsellor. The charge that builds up around an unspoken question is not only a charge between two 'things' in the counsellor's mind, but a charge between the counsellor and the client. It is this inter-personal charge that in turn charges the client's awareness of the absent relation between the two things. When this charge then finally sparks and insight emerges within the client, it is immediately felt in the counselling relationship itself.

It is the irreducible and ineradicable difference between the counsellor's life and experience and that of the client that constitutes the primary charge, tension or 'voltage' of the counselling relationship - and in this sense its central question. For a counsellor to be truly open to the questions raised by a client therefore, is impossible unless they are open to this question - able to experience meaning itself as a still absent, unthought and unspoken relation between what someone communicates or 'means' to us through their words, and what the words they use to do so mean to us. Meaning, in other words, does not have its primary source in Self or Other but in the oscillating dimension of their relation itself - in the charge that gathers in 'the between'. Recognising this means acknowledging also that the explicit questions that clients bring to the counselling session are their individual way of representing shared human questions that are always fundamentally relational in character - for they represent absent or 'negative' relationships that are not yet experienced as absent and thus have not yet built up sufficient charge to spark. Such negative or absent relationships are often experienced instead as positive relationships that have simply gone 'wrong' or that are experienced through emotional negativity. Seen from this point of view the purpose of counselling or therapy is not simply to help clients discover relationships between events and people, nor to explore past or present relationships with a negative character, but rather to help the client to acknowledge and experience *negative relationships* in the literal sense - those *absent relationships* to themselves and others that are the ultimate source of their mental or emotional distress.

These absent relationships are not essentially 'questions' to be answered or 'problems' to be solved. Instead all such explicit personal questions and problems are the expressions of a common human quest - the quest to relate. This quest is the driving force of human life, for were it to be ever finally answered our relational life would be deprived of all creative charge and vitality. Without reverence for the shared and open *mystery* at the heart of every human question - the implicit and experienced questions which can never be fully represented in words and the charge of which can never be fully released - no attempt to 'solve' life's intellectual, emotional and existential 'problems' can succeed *practically* (except through the use of totalitarian or technical solutions which 'work' at the expense of these human relationships). And yet the bias of Western culture is to see dialogue only as a way of 'getting clearer' about relationships between things and people and finding intellectual, emotional, ideological or technical 'answers' or 'solutions'. A dialogue is seen as successful if, instead of going round in circles and leaving everyone no wiser than before, the parties are able to *make* connections or *represent* relationships in a clearer or more sophisticated way. The principal medium for this representation is language.

What I call a 'listening dialogue' is a dialogue with an essentially different direction (telos) and therefore an essentially different character, tone and mood. For a dialogue need not either go round in circles or move towards ever greater explicitness and rational clarity. It can also go deeper in the implicit mystery of the questions it raises, helping each person to take in and experience these questions in a deeper way - not to represent their relationships in words but to actually *relate* in a deeper way. This means experiencing both present and absent relationships more fully, and having the capacity to embody their energy and charge rather than simply discharge this energy in speech. A listening dialogue, one based on withholding verbal questions and reactions, can, paradoxically, help people to represent and understand their relationships with *greater* depth of insight and pragmatic force than an interrogative dialogue that seeks to do this directly - that sacrifices depth of awareness and intensity of charge to the search for clarity and emotional resolution.

Whilst it is accepted that listening is a crucial part of the counsellor's role, rarely does the counselling dialogue take the form of a listening dialogue rather than an interrogative one. The principal medium of the latter is speech. Its goal is verbal explicitness and clarity. Listening is seen only as a means to the end - a tool that helps the counsellor to respond sensitively in words. The medium of a listening dialogue is the intercourse that takes place with others through our listening itself. Its precondition is that our listening does not come to an end when someone has finished speaking but has a chance to deepen in the silence that follows their speech.

It is rarely acknowledged how much the character of a counsellor's listening, its depth and duration, tone and character, itself *sets a tone* that tunes the client's discourse - influencing what they say and how they say it, the length at which they speak and the depths from which they speak, the terms in which they express themselves and the terms in which they don't express themselves. The depth of a client's speech depends on how deeply and with what degree of patience they are able to listen to themselves before speaking. This in turn is influenced by the depth and duration of the counsellor's listening - by which I mean how deeply the counsellor too, is able to listen to themselves before speaking. It is the depth and duration of the counsellor's 'inward listening' therefore, and *not*, merely, as it is usually understood, how attentively they listen and 'attune' to the client that is central to the listening process in counselling.

Many counsellors would be willing to admit that most emotional and relational problems have their source in an unwillingness to listen to ourselves - to heed the inner voice of our feelings - and/or an incapacity to remain in touch with ourselves as we listen to others - the precondition of understanding others from within. From this point of view the very *goal* of counselling is not essentially to give the client an opportunity to speak and be heard as to help them, through the depth and patience of the counsellor's listening, to *listen more deeply to themselves and others*. Yet counselling is still seen and practiced as a type of 'talking cure' rather than as 'listening therapy' in this sense. As a result, the nature and significance of listening as an *inherently* therapeutic process and praxis remains largely unexplored in the 'talking cure'.

Neither the theory nor the practice of counselling fully recognise how much the nature of the counselling dialogue is based on a taboo on *communicative silence* in Western culture. It is this taboo which precludes and inhibits deep listening and therefore contributes to the generation of communicative and interpersonal problems. It goes together with the privileging of verbal responses, questions and the 'talking cure'. But it becomes manifest only in a concealed way - as a deep seated and stubborn resistance to allowing and extending the 'turn interval' between address and response - to permitting oneself an interval of silence before responding to another person in words, or even in non-verbal nods, murmurs and gestures. To gauge the force of this resistance is simple. One need only challenge individuals to delay their spontaneous verbal responses in any conversation, social or professional, even if only for a minimal period of ten seconds or so, in order to see the discomfort and unease - mental, emotional and physical - that this creates. And to suggest to a counsellor - even hypothetically - that they conduct a session with a client without asking any questions (except purely factual ones), and without at any stage echoing or paraphrasing what their clients say to them, creates a similar discomfort. For this may seem to the counsellor (and perhaps is) tantamount to asking them to sacrifice all their acquired helping skills.

In the dialogues of Plato, the provocative and thought-provoking questions that Socrates put to his interlocutors became the explicit model of philosophical dialogue, and the interrogative or 'Socratic' dialogue remains also the implicit model of the counselling dialogue. Socrates himself however, was proud to be the son of a midwife and described his own role as that of a *midwife* to truth. For him this meant helping his interlocutors through his questions to confront and bear the labour pains of thought - and making sure also that their 'firstborn' were more than just 'darling follies'. 'Dire are the pangs which my art is able to arouse and to allay in those who consort with me'. In exercising this role as midwife however, Socrates' first and foremost principle was to listen to the inner voice of his own guiding spirit or *daemon*. Though he provided a forceful and lasting model of the interrogative dialogue, Socrates also modelled a type of listening dialogue. For he himself practised a silent *inward listening* and understood this as the precondition for acting as midwife to the thoughts of others, for to do so meant helping *them* to listen better to themselves.

The type of patient and disciplined withholding from verbal interventions and interrogation that I propose as essential to the deepening of the counselling dialogue is also comparable to the restraint of the patient and forbearing midwife. It is for this reason that I use the term 'maieutic' (from the Greek *maieuesthai* - to act as a midwife) to describe the type of deep listening that alone can bear fruit in the counselling dialogue. To listen maieutically is to adopt a quite different bearing as a listener. It is to bear with others in pregnant silence in such a way as to help them listen more deeply to themselves and allow this silence to bear fruit. Its ultimate aim is not insight or catharsis but rather to help the client to give birth to and embody a new *inner bearing* - a new way of 'carrying' or 'bearing' themselves in everyday life, and thus a new way of 'being-in-the-world' and relating to others. All verbal communication is the expression of an inner bearing. No amount of verbal communication however, can change a person's inner bearing. Helping another to give birth through dialogue requires the adoption of a very specific bearing on the part of the listener - that of the midwife.

The regular and disciplined praxis of maieutic listening through the discipline of withholding can lead the listener to a new and deeper experience of the listening process, and of what it means to really 'hear' someone. This experience is difficult to describe in words, for its essential quality is more akin to the experience of listening deeply to music than to words and speech. It is as if the mental-emotional responses of the listener give way to a response from another place - from the musical soul of the listener. The medium of maieutic listening is not the airy medium of words but the fluid medium of feeling tone - the tones of silence that communicate 'through the word', radiate from the listener and underlie all verbal communication. These may or may not be echoed in the tone of a person's language or their tone of voice. Rather, speech itself may be regarded as a type of song, one that provides a more 'tuned in' expression of the silent music of the soul - the music of feeling tone. Feeling tones are not nameable or expressed 'emotions'. Instead the latter are more like the upsurges of a singer's vocal intensity evoked by language itself and expressed in language itself - in the words of the song. To describe music in terms of verbally nameable and expressible emotions is to confuse musical feeling as such - feeling *tones* - with particular ranges and intensities of feeling that can be named and expressed in feeling *words*. But to understand the deeper, musical dimension of listening requires a deeper understanding of what exactly it means to listen to music itself - to a musician performing or a singer singing.

The playing of a musician and the singing of a singer, like the speaking of a speaker, may be understood as 'expressive' in a visible bodily way as well as in an audible tonal way. But the expressiveness of a musician, of a singer, or of a dancer are expressions not so much of the music itself as of their way of *hearing* that music within themselves. Music is not played as audible tones and then heard by an audience. It is heard in a feeling way - inwardly - and then played. It is the music that is felt and heard inwardly, with its rhythms, harmonies and tones of silence that is the basis of musical composition.

A speaker's speaking, like the composer's marks on a score, a conductor's gestures, a singer's voice or a musician's movements is not simply a form of expression or 'address' that calls for and calls forth a particular *response* from the listener. Instead it is always itself a response conscious or unconscious, tuned or unattuned, to something sensed within - to what I have called the inner music of feeling tone. Attending to so-called 'paralinguistic' features of speech - the speaker's tone of voice and body language, can in no way deepen our listening unless we acknowledge this central truth.

Ordinary listening can be compared to a choral concert in which an orchestra is actually playing in the background but remains unheard by the audience. The audience moreover, concentrates more on the words of the song or the faces of the singers than on the singing itself and the music it responds to. Verbal dialogue can be compared to a gathering of composers, who read aloud the notes of their scores as they compose them, possibly with a musical intonation - *saying* 'A', 'B-flat', 'C' etc. Words, of course also refer to things, events and people. The combinations of notes that they read aloud therefore, also have a meaning that has nothing directly to do with the music. The mental-emotional mind responds to these words rather than to the music which they encode. Though the latter may be echoed in the voice tones of the speaker, these are linked by the listener to the verbal meanings communicated by the words uttered.

Musicians can either play music to one another, play music with one another, or talk about music - to and with one another. But even in verbal communication people are constantly making a type of silent music with one another - whether they are speaking or silent. In making music together, people do not first listen and then play. Their playing itself demands a continuous listening attunement to themselves and the other players. It is itself an expression of this listening attunement. Conversely, listening itself, even in verbal communication, is not merely an attunement to other people's music or a prelude to our own verbal response. Our listening constantly makes its own music, more or less in tune with the music of others. And yet our culture is one characterised by a type of unmusical dialogue in which at worst, people are deaf to the tones of silence on which words ride, and at best only talk about their common music, without at the same time playing it. This is unfortunate, for whilst musicians and singers cannot talk to each other at the same time as they make music together, the inner music of the psyche can be heard and played 'through the word', even whilst talking about something else.

The words 'dialogue' (*dia-logos*) and 'psychology' have their roots in a pre-Socratic understanding of the Greek term logos, not merely as 'word' or 'speech' but as a type of musical inner resonance or reverberation of the *psyche*. That is why the Greek sage Heraclitus could say:

'Not knowing how to listen, neither can they speak.'

For 'men fail to comprehend it (the *logos*) both before hearing it and once they have heard.' Modern 'psychology' seeks to represent the psyche scientifically in words - not to listen to its 'inner word'. The counselling 'dialogue' is also oriented to talking about the psyche - to finding fitting words with which to describe or express feelings rather than responding to those feeling through the logos of the psyche itself - the rich language of feeling tone. Therapists and counsellors may consider it important to attune 'empathically' to the feeling tones communicated through (*dia*) a person's words (*logoi*), but only in order to find fitting words or images for them - not in order to respond to them with and from their own feeling tones --the *logoi* of the *psyche*. This again is unfortunate, for it represents a privileging of verbal over musical dimensions of human psychology, feeling and relating.

As we have already noted, in music making to attune is to 'attone' - to make a tone. The musicians in a quartet do not first attune and then make tones - their playing is a toning attunement, an 'attonement'. Similarly, in human dialogue, we do not simply 'attune' to each other's feeling tones and respond to them with our own. Instead the wavelengths on which we attune to other people's feelings each carry their own tone. Feeling tones are the silent tones of our listening - modulated by the wavelengths on which we tune in to ourselves and others. Our listening attunement to ourselves and others is the inner music we make. The listener does not simply attend to sound. Listening is also a 'sounding out'.

Listening with the musical soul is therefore impossible if we see our role merely as that of a detached observer of other people's psyches, driven by curiosity about the different types of soul music that people have and hear within them, and that they seek to communicate and express. It represents a qualitatively different experience of what it means to really 'hear' someone and to 'see' what they are saying, one that is usually only experienced in a very intense and rich way in listening to music. We hear music fully only when we resonate and respond to it inwardly, with the music of our own souls. What we are able to 'see' with our musical ear when we listen to another person speak emerges in a different way and in a different sort of time than the thoughts, emotions and images evoked by their words. Put in other terms, what is pregnant in a dialogue takes time to mature. It is never fully born in words even though it is borne through them. And it is always the product of the dialogical relation itself, of a mutual music making.

The maieutic listener does not contrive only to support others through emotional labour and to give birth in speech, whilst remaining detached or totally silent themselves. Nor does maieutic listening mean taking on the whole burden of another person's psychological pregnancy and bringing it to fruition in oneself. The maieutic listener is a midwife to the dialogue and of the dialogical relationship itself, able to tolerate the charge of its unspoken questions. It would be absurd for listeners at a concert to halt the performance and indulge in questioning or talking 'about' the music every time the felt questions it gave expression to built up charge.

Styles of therapy or counselling which substitute talk for an inner musical responsiveness to others run the risk of reducing themselves to equal absurdity; using questions to fill in missing pieces of a jigsaw puzzle, or using interpretations to supply them - rather than letting the whole picture appear, with its holes. Or, using the musical analogy - letting the whole symphony play with its natural intervals and pauses, its charged silences and their inner tones. Only with this attitude can the counsellor transform the counselling dialogue into a genuinely questioning and listening dialogue. Only in this way can he or she learn the art of *conducting* the counselling dialogue in an attuned and musical way, and not merely with words and questions. There is a telepathic dimension to this way of engaging in a dialogue, one which recognises the telepathic dimension of all communication, verbal and non-verbal.

Psychoanalysis, whilst recognising this dimension to a certain extent, nevertheless paints it in a negative light. Telepathy and psychic powers are associated with infantile 'omnipotence' fantasies - the belief that one can read other people's thoughts, influence or be influenced by them. This association rests on a fundamental misinterpretation of telepathy as 'thought transference' or 'thought reading', a misinterpretation that also governs scientific parapsychology and its experiments in thought transmission. On top of this, psychoanalysis adds its own concept of 'projective identification', one which implies that internal psychic elements or 'part objects' of the self can be transferred from one person to another. Both the idea of 'thought transference' and the notion of 'object transference' imply that telepathy has to do with the movement of 'things' - thoughts, feelings or mental images - from one person to another. The maieutic understanding of telepathy, on the other hand, is not based on any concept of transference but on the dynamics of perceptual interactivity. The way we perceive other people is always perceived or, 'picked up' by them, whether consciously or unconsciously, and irrespective of whether we verbalise or express our perceptions or not. This direct telepathic awareness is not a product of thought or feeling transference but arises from the very nature of perception. 'Every act of perception alters both perceiver and perceived.' (Seth). In the case of human interaction the perceived, however, is also a perceiver. Our perception of the way another person perceives us, therefore, in turn acts on the person perceiving us. Human interaction is thus a 'non-linear' field of dynamic 'inter-activity' between mutually perceiving subjects. Identifiable 'objects' of consciousness are not transferred between psyches. They are themselves expressions of this psychic field of interactivity between beings, the interface of perception. The way I see another person may communicate through the look on my face or the look in my eyes for example. This does not mean that the other person can only pick up my way of seeing them by scrutinising my face and eyes and 'interpreting' its objective features. For as soon as one person's body, face or eyes becomes a *mere* object of perception to the other person they are no longer looking at or perceiving the person. If an optician looks at my eyes, for example, they are precisely not looking at or seeing me. Where there is objectification and interpretation of the other person there is no longer any true relation, nor any true perception of the other as a being - a 'you'. This has enormous implications for our understanding of listening and hearing. As Martin Heidegger so succinctly put it: '*We* hear, not the ear.'

Perception is essentially not a subject-object relation but a direct relation of beings, of an 'I' and a 'you'. Objective perception of 'body language' in the form of facial expression, eye signals, posture and gestures etc., are not an indirect 'expression' of interhuman communication but the most direct *embodiment* of that communication.

The telepathic character of the level of silent inner communication explored through maieutic listening has already been referred to. It is hinted at by expressions such as 'being on someone's wavelength' or 'tuning in'. For just as every act of perception acts on the perceived, so does the wavelength on which we attune to another person's feelings also carry and convey its own specific 'feeling tone'. The wavelengths of our feeling attunement to others are themselves feeling tones which *set a tone* - affecting all that is said and heard. Such wavelengths of attunement are also 'carrier waves' on which messages can be telepathically 'received' by the listener. They also carry a message from the listener to the speaker, setting the 'ground tone' for a dialogue and setting the tone for what will be said and heard. The active telepathic communication explored in maieutic listening occurs through modulating and varying the tone of our listening, whilst at the same time being aware that all such modulations and variations of our listening tone are picked up by the speaker. We do not listen to people because they are speaking to us. People speak to us, and speak to us in a particular way about particular things, because they are aware that we are open or not open to listening in a particular way. Where speaking is part of a dialogue and not a monologue, it is always an expression of and a response to particular ways of listening - the ways we listen to ourselves and the ways others listen to us.

In the last analysis there is no such thing as a pure monologue, for speech is always, even if implicitly, both an address and a response to a 'you'. Dialogue can become monotonal however. The counsellor as listener may seek a type of 'rapport' in which the tone of their listening and of their language is never in contrast with the tone of the client's speech or comportment. This sort of 'echoing' or 'mirroring' however, sets up a type of dialogue which is essentially monological and monotonal.

Maieutic listening follows instead the guidance of Heraclitus: 'From tones at variance comes perfect attunement'. The tonal modulation of the counsellor's listening in responding inwardly to the client, like the tonal modulation of the counsellor's voice in addressing the client outwardly, is not an arbitrary modulation but a musically tuned one - sensitive to the different tonal textures and layers of the dialogue itself. It attempts to create a common music - one that does justice to the different wavelengths of thought, feeling, being and relating that are native to both client and counsellor and that express their fundamental 'tones of being'. This silent tonal communication is the telepathic basis of genuine insight - the perception of relationships in thought. Western culture values music and there are many who appreciate it as a more richly differentiated medium than verbal language - not only as an expression of feelings but as a medium of thought, intuition and imagination. Yet Western psychology remains stuck in the notion that pre-verbal awareness is 'undifferentiated' - that without words our experience and identity itself lack internal differentiation and distinctions. In fact any medium of aesthetic perception and creation is also a medium of thought, for it opens up a perception of relationships. The converse is not the case however. Not all types of thinking open up a perception of relationships. For the way we perceive relationships *between* things and *between* people affects and is affected by our way of relating to them.

Genuine and profound insights into relationships *between* people both arise from and help bring about a deeper, more profound way of relating *to* them.

Deeper modes of relating to others are nourishing and energising. For in the last analysis 'energy' is only what outwardly 'relates', 'connects' or 'binds' beings with one another. It is not outer energy that relates us as beings but deep inner relating that energises us - putting us in touch with our own core self and linking it with the core selves of others. That is why a deepened sense of inner connection with others can release so much energy - like the vast energies released by fusion of the nuclear core of hitherto separate atoms.

'To love' and 'to feel' are both verbs. Love is not 'a feeling' but the activity of feeling and receiving another through which deep inner connection is established. In this way loving can also be a source of deep thinking and insight into others. But establishing deep inner connection is not the same thing as 'making connections' in one's mind. Similarly, sharing insights into relationships with others is not the same thing as actually relating to others on a deep level - and helping others to do so.

What the listening counsellor listens for is not evident outer connections between elements of a client's discourse or narrative but *absence*s of connection. It is such absences of connection or outright contradictions that give clues not only to unconnected aspects of the client's psyche but to their felt lack of inner connection to themselves and others. It is these absences of connection that also constitute the true 'question' - the question that is felt but as yet unformulated, for its essence lies in a felt absence of relation of connection. A mere well-intentioned desire on the part of a counsellor to 'connect' with the client and 'make connections' from what they say can actually hinder this type of deep listening - a listening that hearkens to absences of inner connection and absence of inner relation or inner connectedness - and that allows both to be *felt* as questions before any attempt is made to formulate those questions.

Connections 'seen' or 'made' in the counsellor's mind do not in themselves alter a client's way of relating to themselves or others. Deep insights on the other hand do not need to be imposed on or 'applied' by the client in order to effect 'real' change. For they are themselves the expression of a change brought about through the counsellor's capacity to connect with the client on a deeper level and *feel* the inner connections and sense of connectedness hitherto *unfelt* by the client. It is not the mere formulation of those connections or the striving to outwardly 'connect' with the client that counts. What counts is the counsellor's *feeling awareness* of connections unfelt by the client. For this feeling awareness is what *touches* the client in silence and what first establishes true inner contact with them. Only by withholding from all attempts to 'connect' with the client or 'make connections' can the counsellor focus instead on felt absences of connection or connectedness with the client. Only in this way can the counsellor touch and transform the client directly with their feeling awareness as well as formulating this awareness in words.

THE LISTENER AS MIDWIFE

An Introduction to Maieutic Listening

Introduction

What I call 'maieutic listening' is a therapeutic listening praxis grounded in phenomenological research into the nature of the listening process. There are many questions still unasked regarding the nature and aims of psychotherapy, the role of listening in the therapeutic relationship, and, above all why the nature and psychology of listening as such still has no place in the theoretical or practical syllabus of different schools of psychotherapy training. Why, despite the central importance of listening in the practice of therapy and the therapeutic process, have phenomenological explorations of the therapist's own listening process and praxis been neglected or marginalised? This essay introduces the philosophical background and ethical foundations of listening as a direct medium of therapeutic interaction, relating these both to the broad framework of 'psychotherapy' and to the practice of 'bodywork' therapies in particular. It is impossible, within the confines of this article, to give a complete account of the phenomenological foundations of maieutic listening, its developmental history and its results in psychotherapy. I will therefore concentrate to begin with on sketching its ethical and philosophical foundations. These are then fleshed out with an elaboration of key metaphors that link maieutic listening with touch therapies and bodywork. The metaphorical language that is employed should be understood not merely as the statement of a theoretical position, but an attempt to communicate in as resonant a way as possible new experiential dimensions of the listening process.

Historical Roots

Maieutic listening has its principal roots in the thinking of the German philosopher Martin Heidegger and the relational ethics of Martin Buber. Heidegger's influence on existential psychotherapy is well known, as is the influence of Buber's work 'I and Thou' on person-centred counselling and integrative psychotherapy. Bringing the contributions of these two major thinkers together is not an easy task. Heidegger's emphasis on the human being's relationship to Being contrasts with Buber's emphasis on the relational dimension of the human being and the relationships of human beings to one another. The former understood the essence of the human being as a relation to something that was not itself anything human - thus offering a fundamental challenge to humanism. Buber's own recognition of the individual's spiritual relation to a divine as well as a personal 'Thou' on the other hand, has been neglected in psychological literature. Both thinkers were insistent, however, that the essence of the human being could not be reduced to an object or 'It', whether it be called 'the unconscious' or 'the self', 'libido' or 'energy'. Both thinkers also understood listening as something far more than a mere natural ability, communicative skill or empathic gift, realising that it was (a) the most basic expression of our capacity to *relate* to our inner being and other human beings, and (b) that it held the secret to wordless dimensions of meaning and being that can never be fully represented *in* words but communicate in a subtle and metaphorical way *through* the word (*dia-logos*).

The Philosophy of Maieutic Listening

The philosophical foundation of maieutic listening is the understanding of the *human* being as the human embodiment of a *being* that is not itself essentially human. This being is not a 'person', even the 'whole person', nor is it an *in*human entity or an impersonal energy, cosmic or divine. It is both the source of our humanity and personhood in all its aspects, and our innermost *being*. The whole *human being* is not the person - a partially or wholly integrated self or 'I', but a 'We' - a living relationship between the person and their inner being. It is the spiritual depth and intimacy of this relationship that determines the person's capacity to listen and relate to *others* in an intimate way - not simply as human beings but as human expressions of their own inner, and larger being. Modern culture acknowledges only two types of intimacy - emotional intimacy achieved through talk, and physical intimacy through touch. Maieutic listening is the cultivation of a third mode of intimacy. This is a spiritual intimacy achieved through inner *listening* contact with others. It has the character of a direct and unmediated I-Thou relation, except that this relation is understood not in Martin Buber's terms - as a relation of two persons - but as a relation of two people to their own and each other's inner being. As a person I can only fully relate to the other as a Thou by first learning to relate to my own inner being as something *other* than my own 'I'. By relating to it as an inner Thou. That is because our inner being cannot be reduced to an object or 'It' or even to an 'I' - an inner Self. For the nature of this inner or 'core' self is precisely that it is *other* than the self we know, and in this sense a Thou rather than an 'I'. Only when our personal self or 'I' links itself to this inner Thou and forms an intimate 'We', do we become whole human beings - able to listen and relate to others as whole human beings. It is the relation between the 'I' and this inner 'Thou', the way they form - or do not form - a We, that is the focus of maieutic listening, and not just the person and their interpersonal relationships, past or present. The person's individual relation to their inner being is essentially a listening relationship. It can be heard through their use of language and the way they talk *about* themselves, but it cannot itself be thematised or talked about - made into an object of literal language. It can however be sensed in a bodily way and understood in a feeling way through the basic metaphors of maieutic listening.

Maieusis as Spiritual Midwifery

The term 'maieutic' comes from the Greek *maieuesthai* - to act as a midwife. Listening, not only to others but to ourselves, is the midwife of speech. One peculiarity of the midwife's role, however, is that she not only tends a person, the mother, but needs to attend and attune to a dyad, the mother and the spirit of the unborn child she carries or 'bears'. The 'We' that can be formed between the 'I' and the inner Thou is comparable to the 'We' formed between a pregnant mother and her unborn child. As human beings we are born, age and die. Our inner being, on the other hand, though far from being a baby, is forever unborn. At the same time it is the fount of all our life potentials, potentials which can never be fully embodied or expressed in any one lifetime however 'whole' or 'integrated' we become. Maieutic listening distinguishes between 'personality', the way we bear and body forth these potentials, personifying them in word and deed, and 'character', our capacity to bear and embody these potentials in stillness and silence, allowing them to mature within us through a listening process. The aim of maieutic listening is the broadening of personality and the deepening of character, not only the emotional integration of different sides of our personality, but the deepening of our inner relation to their ever-pregnant source. Deepening character means learning to continuously bear the true weight and wonder of our inner being, just as a pregnant mother bears the weight and the wonder of the baby growing within her. But just as being pregnant, despite its discomforts and symptoms is essentially distinct from being ill or giving birth, so is *bearing* essentially distinct from repressively containing, cathartically evacuating or passively 'suffering'.

Psychotherapy and Religion

The relation between suffering and bearing is at the heart of many of humanity's deepest religious metaphors, in particular those Christian metaphors to do with the birth of Christ from the Virgin as the fleshly incarnation of the Father. The confusion between suffering and bearing, healing and giving birth is the source of those misconceived forms of psychotherapeutic practice that seek a conquest of human suffering which alleviates all need for bearing. There is a pseudo-Christian and evangelical theology at the heart of such practices, holding out the promise of a final triumphant birth or rebirth of the personal self or 'I' in which the inner Thou is subsumed and disappears - for its human potentials are now fully realised or incarnate. Such an incarnation of the realised Self would abolish the tension of an ongoing *relation* to the inner Thou, to others and otherness. This stance, however mistaken or inaccurate in strict theological terms, is reflected in all sorts of ways in the self-understanding of psychotherapy and its aims, which focuses one-sidedly on the importance of emotional 'labour' or 'work' and what this work can give birth to (albeit with accompanying labour pains) rather than on the ongoing tension of *bearing* what is as-yet unborn and giving it time to ripen and mature in silence. Both talking and touching therapies, analysis and bodywork reflect theology, sharing a common language to do with 'working on' and 'working through' issues, 'bringing up' buried memories or blocked energies, 'releasing' psychological and bodily tensions. Crudely exaggerated, this is comparable to a type of midwifery in which the whole nine months of pregnancy were of no consequence, and it was believed that delivery could, with the right skills and techniques, be facilitated at any time. How much of therapeutic practice is in fact a type of gentle but nevertheless premature and in this sense forced attempt at delivery by the midwife? More importantly, how much does it collude with the client's own fear of what is still pregnant within them, their anxiety to name and objectify it, abort or cathart it - in a word, their desire to deliver themselves of it with the aid of the therapist qua midwife?

Bearing and Birthing

The relation of mother and foetus is a relation between a self giving birth and the self yet to be born. Through the metaphorical language of bearing we can understand the inner Thou as the non-human or spiritual 'father' of this self, able to fertilise the seeds of change planted by life experience and events. The 'I' or personal self is its human mother. The body its psychological womb. The foetus is its felt presence within that womb. When we allow ourselves to feel feelings that previously seemed unbearable, we become mothers to ourselves, able to bear these feelings in the womb of our bodily experience, and give them time to mature. When these bodied feelings begin to transform our felt sense of who we are, we give birth to ourselves. From the point of view of the mother self, the birth process is like dying - an experience of releasing the body from the hold of the personal 'I' and releasing an infantile self from our bodies. From the point of view of the self that is born, however, the birthing process is quite the opposite - an experience of incarnation in which we enter our bodies in a new way or feel an older, more mature self come into them. This self is an *incarnation* of the father in the body of the mother.

Listening and Psychotherapy Training

Therapists who are trained only to facilitate and respond to the client's speech but who are unable to bear the pregnant silence that precedes, follows or pervades this speech are not *listening* therapists in the true sense, however empathically responsive they may be. Such therapists will rely on their own training to provide them with a framework of theoretical knowledge and technical skills for understanding and 'working on' the client's issues. For them, listening will be understood merely as an important and necessary prelude to providing some sort of helpful therapeutic response, whether in the form of talk or touch, verbal intervention or bodywork. The model is simple: the client talks freely, the therapist listens and responds 'empathically' to the best of their ability and in a way that conforms to their professional training. What is missing in this model is an understanding that what a client says and the way they say it is already a response to the way the therapist is listening - to where they are listening from and what they are listening for, to wavelengths of empathic attunement that are available to them and those which are not, to their patience or impatience as listeners, and above all, to their acquired ways of construing what they hear, something which is often anticipated in the client's speech. A therapist who is unaware of how they are listening and of their own listening process cannot distinguish their own inner responses and perceptions from responses and perceptions acquired in the course of their professional training. In other words, they cannot distinguish what they hear from what they have been *trained* to hear, and the ways they have been trained to construe their own perceptions. Nor can they distinguish their own inner responses to a client, from the ways they have been trained to interpret these inner responses and translate them into outer responses. Above all, they may be quite unaware that their inner listening response to a client communicates quite independently of whatever words they dress it in or whatever outer responses they give or do not give. Alternatively, they may be very well aware of all this, and yet find it a source of anxiety and troubling unclarity about what is really going on in the therapeutic relationship. Part of this anxiety may itself be a product of their training, above all where the latter does not give a central place to understanding the nature of listening and the listening process, and reinforces common myths about it.

Listening and Feeling

Inward listening is what gives us time to feel our feelings in a wordless and bodily way, without needing to release, express or repress them, indeed without even needing to name or reflect on them. Naming and discussing feelings in words, on the other hand, turns them into felt thoughts, feelings we interpret mentally as being *about* something or *towards* someone. It is not feelings per se, but emotionally charged thoughts that we express or repress, fight or flee from, or get so stuck in that we freeze emotionally, cutting ourselves off from all bodily feeling. Most forms of counselling and psychotherapy share a culture of 'emotional literacy' which encourages people to name and describe their feelings - to talk about them. This culture appears to run counter to the 'intellectualisation', 'acting out' or 'somatisation' of feelings. In practice, however, it can represent a type of imperialism of the intellect, for asking a client to name or describe a feeling demands that they intellectually detach from it, turning it into an internal mental object. At the same time it transforms the bodily feeling into a felt *thought* - a feeling 'about' or 'towards' an object. Talking to someone about our feelings is quite different in principle from speaking to someone in an authentic way - speaking *with* feeling and from our feelings. Authentic speech communicates feelings *through* our words and body language rather than trying to define and represent them *in* words or express them in physical gestures. Talking about feelings is like talking about music. We are limited by the vocabulary of the 'emotions' such as 'hurt' or 'disappointment', 'anger' or 'joy', a vocabulary which can never do justice to the full range of our feeling *tones* and what they themselves communicate - not verbally but *musically*. The paradox of psychotherapeutic discourse is that far from generating emotional 'literacy' it can easily result in an impoverishment of emotional language. More importantly, getting a client to talk *about* their feelings can prevent them from speaking *with* feeling about the issues that really concern them.

Listening Speech and Listening Dialogue

A poet seeking to communicate their intense feeling experience of a landscape does not write about their feelings but about the landscape itself. Nature itself provides the poet with a rich metaphorical language for communicating their feelings, a language far more apposite and less limited than a literalistic language of named and labelled emotions. Similarly, speaking with feeling about the issues that concern us we are less limited by the vocabulary of the emotions - the issues themselves provide a far broader range of implicit metaphors. Ultimately, the difference between a purely intellectual discourse and a speech imbued with deep feeling has nothing to do with the topical focus of that discourse (e.g. whether it is about feelings or not), but with the type of listening that is midwife to it. Feeling speech is reflective, meditative speech - listening speech. A feeling speech, rooted in inward listening, is also a genuinely thoughtful speech - one that listens inwardly for the apposite words and metaphors rather than relying on stereotyped language and thought patterns. The new and more profound thoughts and insights that lie pregnant in our feelings cannot be brought to expression by merely naming those feelings in words. They must first be given time to incubate and gestate. Listening is what grants us time to feel our feelings in a wordless way, to incubate the thoughts that are pregnant within them, and find the words that will truly communicate them.

The Discipline and Inner Stance of Maieutic Listening

The aim of maieutic listening is to create the conditions for a feeling and thoughtful speech and therefore also for a genuine listening dialogue in which feelings are communicated *dia-logos* - 'through the word' rather than in words. The basic inner discipline of maieutic listening is the withholding of the spoken word, not just while another person is speaking but before and after they speak. It is through this discipline that we strengthen our capacity to bear with others in silence, sharing with them the task of bearing the feelings that lie pregnant in silence. The basic inner stance of the maieutic listener is a stance of *forbearance*. Forbearance does not mean stoically tolerating, containing or 'suffering' difficult and intense feelings but giving them time to mature and bear fruit, giving birth to new insights and a new sense of self. To embody this stance however, means not merely being aware of feelings 'in' our bodies but having the courage to feel them with our whole body - to body them. Bodily feelings that we experience as independent 'energies' arising in a part of our body, feelings that disturb our minds or express themselves as discomforting somatic sensations and symptoms are feelings that we have not yet *fully* bodied, fully identified with in a bodily way. But when we allow ourselves to feel the feeling with our whole body then it ceases to be a purely bodily feeling. *We* feel - not the body or mind. Then we do not need to contain or release, express or repress our feelings because they begin to change us, altering our sense of self and changing into other feelings as they do so. The work of the maieutic listener, the work of forbearance, is a work of bodying feelings. It is therefore essentially a bodily work or 'bodywork', but one of a quite different character to the type of therapeutic work that normally goes under this name. The latter takes as its starting point the experience of emotionally charged 'energies' in a part or parts of our body, and aims at the release and expression of these emotional energies which are otherwise thought of as being 'trapped' or 'blocked' by emotional armouring.

Listening That Works

Maieutic listening understands feelings not as 'emotional energies' but as pregnant meanings, meanings which we are not yet able to communicate, because to do so we must first allow ourselves to feel them. The less we are able to feel these meanings with our whole body and whole self, the more we experience them as emotional energies connected with a part of ourselves and felt in a part or parts of our body. The word energy derives from the Greek *energein* - 'to work'. To talk of working 'with' or 'on' someone's energy is therefore somewhat tautological. But if the therapist is able to listen with forbearance, to help the client bear their feelings by bearing them with the client, then the therapist's listening will indeed work in quite profound ways. Released from the need to repress or express, contain or evacuate their feelings, yet sensing that the therapist is prepared not only to acknowledge them but to share in bearing them, the client's bodily defences will begin to relax without any direct touch or 'bodywork'. The therapist's capacity to body these feelings without rigidifying or contracting, without catharting or acting out, without turning them into mental objects or manipulating them as bodily energies, will help the client to feel safe. The therapist will be silently modelling - embodying - a different way of being with and communicating feelings, one that the client will sense in a bodily way and begin to learn from.

Therapy and Transformation

Maieutic listening is not a set of ideas about human suffering and its causes, nor a set of techniques for overcoming it, but an inner stance or 'bearing' quite distinct from that cultivated in both analysis and bodywork, existential and integrative psychotherapy. It requires a deep and mature capacity for forbearance, to bear with others in silence, whatever the intensity of feelings that lie pregnant in this silence. And yet it is this alone that helps others to feel their feelings in a bodily way - to bear and body them. Doing so transforms their suffering into a new inner bearing on life. By this I mean a new bodily feeling of who they are, one through which they both discover and embody new aspects of their inner being. Many people come to therapy because they want desperately to change *the way they feel*, but do not know what it means to be changed *by their feelings*. Talking about feelings and searching for their meaning is one way of distancing ourselves from them, making sure that what we feel does not affect our sense of self - who we feel ourselves to be. The very formula 'I feel X' implies an unchanging subject or 'I' whose identity remains the same whatever this 'I' feels. But the meaning pregnant in a feeling is nothing that can be teased out by psychoanalysis. Instead it has to do with the way this feeling can alter our sense of self in a quite bodily way - if we allow it to permeate our bodies. Change does not result from insight into feelings. Insight accompanies or follows a felt bodily sense of becoming other - a transformation in one's bodily sense of self. Maieutic listening is *therapeutic* listening because it is transformative listening - listening which changes both therapist and client. It is not merely a prelude to finding some sort of therapeutic response to the client that will then 'help' the client to change. The therapist's own embodied presence works quite directly on the client, helping them to feel a bodily link between their outer, personal self on the one hand, and the felt but as-yet unborn potentials of their inner being on the other. Their attunement to the client's inner being is an attunement to an as-yet unheard and silent voice. In listening to the client, the therapist is aware that the voice that speaks is one voice only, and beneath it is a deeper more authentic voice. If a client begins to embody important changes they will begin to speak from a different place within themselves and in a different voice - a quite different matter from merely thinking or talking *about* themselves in different way. One of the paradoxes of the change process is that the voice that announces changes and talks about them is often the voice of the *unchanged* self. When someone says 'I have changed', the 'I' is often that of this unchanged self, one that still has not fully identified with the changes it reports, but keeps them at a distance by objectifying them. Just as the midwife attunes to two selves - a self giving birth and a self being born, so is the maieutic listening of the therapist sensitive to the twin voices of the client - that of the self that is changing and that of the changed self. Whenever a change has been completed, the individual no longer has the same need to speak about this change in their old voice - instead he or she will embody the change, speaking from their changed self rather than about it. The new place they speak from is a new inner bearing with its own inner tone and vocal resonance. The therapist will hear the changes in tone and language that signal the birth of this new voice. If not, it is all the more important that the therapist remains attuned to a voice that is as-yet unheard, one that fully embodies the changes desired - or already described - by the client.

Listening and Core Contact

Listening maieutically, the therapist's whole physical bearing will embody and communicate a different way of being with others - a capacity to meet and be met, touch and be touched, address and respond to other beings on a 'core' level, quite independently of any physical touch or verbal talk. Making contact with the client as a being means more than establishing a good professional rapport with the person. A good interpersonal rapport can exist even where there is no real meeting of beings. For this to happen the therapist requires a deep groundedness in their own being, and an ability to inwardly lean or list their being towards the client - to *list-en*. What I call core contact with others is not made with the body but only through it. The fact that I look at your eyes, communicate feelings or exchange emotional signals through them does not mean that I make genuine eye contact - that I see *you* rather than your physical eyes and their emotional radiance. To do so I must be fully present in my own gaze, not only as a feeling human person but as a spiritual being. The fact that I listen to you with my head and my heart does not mean that I hear *you* - the inner being or Thou. To do so *I* must be fully present to myself, in touch with my own inner being, and attuned to its inner voice. When a woman is pregnant she learns to adjust her physical posture in order to accommodate her increased weight and enlarged belly. Her centre of bodily awareness lowers itself to the belly region, in response to its weight and the pull of gravity. Listening maieutically means allowing ourselves to respond to the gravitational pull of deep feelings, lowering the centre of consciousness from the head or the heart to what we call the 'guts' and what the Japanese call *hara*. *Hara* is not only our body's physical centre of gravity but its spiritual centre of gravity too - the place of deep inner silence where our embodied human self meets the inner human being. After birth we are no longer in the womb. But whether male or female there is a womb within us. This is the inner womb of silence, filled not with amniotic waters but with tones of silence - the fluid medium of feeling tone. The umbilical cord reaches deep inside the womb to the body of the foetus. Listening maieutically feels rather like extending an umbilical cord to a still point of silence in the belly - the *hara* - entering that silence and allowing it to inwardly expand like a womb. In making core contact with others it can feel as if there is an invisible fibre of energy issuing from a point just below the navel. This fibre is extended by our intent. We *attend* to a person, their words and body language, their thoughts and feelings. To make core contact with another being we must *intend* them - *mean* to hear the being and not just the person. In doing so we extend a tendril of intent that reaches out towards them from the still point of silence within the listening body, touching them not from without but from within. Core contact, whether through the ears, eyes or hands, through hearing, sight or touch, is always in its essence an inner listening contact. It is analogous to the midwife's use of a stethoscope placed on the mother's belly, forging as it does a type of inner umbilical contact which allows something - or rather *someone* - to be heard.

Listening and Inner Touch

When we speak metaphorically of being 'touched' by an event, 'holding on' to someone, or having a 'broken heart' we are not simply using bodily metaphors - body language - to describe emotional states. Nor are we speaking literally of the physical body. We are speaking of a body - a metaphysical body. The metaphysical body is the soul body or psychic body - the body that is touched by an event because it means something to us. Conversely, a soul is nothing more nor less than a being capable of meaning something. A computer can give us information but it does not mean anything with that information nor does it mean the being it gives it to. Human beings are capable of meaning someone as well as meaning something - intending another being. The metaphysical body is the body of meaning, the body with which we mean and feel meaning. Emotional energy is the physical 'working' of meaning. The physical body is a living biological metaphor of the metaphysical body - our body of meaning. Meaning, conversely, is metaphysical energy - the direct energy or 'working' of intent. To touch a person's body with the intent to 'work on their energy' is not the same thing as to intend to touch the human being. 'Working on their energy' may affect the person but it will not necessarily touch their inner being. But if our intent is to touch a being and not just their physical body, this intent will itself work metaphysically, and be experienced energetically.

When we touch someone's flesh we feel its contours, warmth, and texture. For a sensitive masseuse, feeling another person's body allows them to receive a message, tells them something about the human being. But their touch also bears back a message to this human being. Massaging is also messaging. It has a *re-lational* dimension, in the original sense of this word, which means 'to bear back a message'. The way we listen to what someone says also bears back a message - says something to them and touches them. Listening is not just the way we understand what someone means - the message they are conveying to us. It is a way of *meaning* something to them, conveying a message to them. It is not merely a passive or receptive mode of verbal communication. It is an active mode of silent, wordless communication - 'core communication' based on core contact.

Listening and Core Communication

Just as we convey countless wordless messages to others through our tones of voice, so do we also convey messages through tones of silence - the tones of our listening. Feelings are essentially tones of being, embodied in muscle tone and expressed as vocal tone. Feeling tones have an intrinsically relational character, for they are also the very wavelengths of attunement by which we connect with other beings. Every listener not only enters into a greater or lesser degree of *resonance* with the feeling tones of others. The listener also *sets* a tone in the very act of attuning to others *on* a particular wavelength - one which may be more or less in resonance with the basic feeling tone of the other. In maieutic listening, the therapist is aware that the silent *tone* of their listening is something they can actively modulate, and that like a person's tone of voice it serves as a 'carrier wave' on which subtle messages ride. The maieutic listener is aware too, that the subtlest modulation of their 'inner voice' - the tone of their listening - bears its own message to the client, attuning the client to themselves in a different way. A useful analogy here is sonar. Through the tone of our listening we can 'sound out' and search the soul of another, but in doing so we also touch them in a tangible, bodily way with the specific vibrational tone of our listening. Maieutic listening can be described as a form of 'inner voice communication' that is at the same time a medium of 'inner vibrational touch'.

'Feelings' are something we 'have'. *Feeling* is something we do - as when we feel an object with our hands. In doing so we also touch that object. In touching another with the tone of our listening we not only become sensitive to their 'feelings'. We *feel* the other, and thereby also touch them with the tone of our feeling awareness. Just as a rough or gentle tone of voice will touch the other in a rougher or gentler way, so does every modulation of the amplitude, tempo, tone and timbre of our inner voice - the tone of our listening. We can learn not only to experience listening as a medium of inner messaging but as a type of inner touch or massage.

Just as we can feel massaged by the mellowness of a person's outer voice so can we feel massaged by the inner voice of a listener. Just as our bodily voice has its own tonal range, so does our inner or listening voice. The whole art of maieutic listening lies in learning to actively modulate the inner tone of our listening, in the same way that we might modulate the tone of our outer voice. Many therapists are aware of the tone of voice they adopt with clients, the messages this may convey and what it may indirectly reveal of their own unspoken thoughts and feelings. They are generally far less aware however, that these private and personal thoughts and feelings also communicate directly and wordlessly to the client. They do so by riding on and modulating the tone of their listening voice in the same way that spoken words ride on and modulate their speaking voice.

Whereas our speaking voice has a limited range, the tonal range of our listening voice is not limited. By entering the still point of silence, we can attune to unutterable tones of being far deeper than those connected with the personal self and its surface emotional responses to others. The maieutic listener first of all seeks attunement to this 'fundamental tone'. Anchoring their listening in this deep and primal tone of their own being is what allows them to make core contact with the inner being of others. The vocal communication that goes on between client and therapist, together with the interpersonal and emotional interactions it expresses, are then both experienced as echoes and translations of a yet deeper contact and communication.

Dying to the Mask

The discipline and basic stance of maieutic listening, that of withholding outward responses in order to bear with others in pregnant silence, is what allows the therapist to make contact with the client on a core level, bearing back their inner responses to the latter as messages borne on tones of silence. Those messages communicate to the client on a core level, and may be experienced as a type of inner vibrational touch or massage. The aim and value of maieutic listening lies in helping others to body their own feelings and the unborn aspects of their being that lie pregnant within them. For the listener themselves, however, adopting the maieutic stance means ceasing to identify with their personal self, the mask or 'persona' through which they normally respond (*per-sonare* - to sound through). This personal self is not merely a set of strong psychological identifications. It is the body of all those mental and emotional, organic and muscular reactions which work together in the activity of speech - the speaking body or 'personality'. The purpose of withholding is to disidentify from the ordinary personality and speaking self. The bodily experience of entering the maieutic stance is one of temporarily letting go of this self and its body - dying to it - and letting all its emotional and muscular reactions die down and die away. We let the speaking body die away and die down towards the core of our being. This in turn brings about a temporary inner relaxation or 'melting' of what Reich called 'character armouring', something which the personality itself, the speaking body and its mask, constantly serves to reproduce and reinforce.

The Two Positions of the Ego

'Spirit is a fundamentally tuned, knowing resolve towards the essence of being.' (Martin Heidegger) Maieutic listening has a deeply spiritual character, being a resolved and intentional attunement to the fundamental tone of our own innermost being. Our ego and personal self are not surrendered in entering the basic spiritual bearing or posture of maieutic listening. Instead it is our own ego which must knowingly resolve to *intend* such a posture - to both maintain the discipline of withholding and to attune and 'intend' our Inner Thou. It is our ego in turn, that is spiritually strengthened and transformed by this process, moving from what Melanie Klein called the 'paranoid-schizoid' position to the 'depressive position'. From an existential perspective, the 'paranoid-schizoid' position is the position from which our ego adopts an I-It relation to both our bodies and our inner being, turning both mind and body, sensations and feelings into external or internal objects that we own as 'self' or disown as 'other'. The contrast between this position and the depressive position was well described by Winnicott as a contrast between 'reacting' (what bodyworkers call the 'startle' response to external impingements) and 'going on being'. The movement from ordinary listening to maieutic listening is a movement from a listening in which the ego descends from the paranoid-schizoid position and sinks to a 'depressive position' - one *grounded* in its inner being. A movement from reacting and acting out to 'going on being', from seeking an external response to others - something to do or say - to feeling our inner responses and bodying those responses, from a hearing shaped by the verbal mind and speaking body to a listening which is tuned to the ear of our inner being and embodies its silent voice. This movement is, I believe the healing essence of the depressive process.

Looking and Listening

In ordinary interpersonal communication, lack of outward responsiveness, and the avoidance of eye-contact with others is taken as a sign of unresponsiveness or even pathology. In therapy too, the warm, spontaneous and 'responsive' practitioner is often counterposed to the cool, analytic one. The maieutic stance is based on the understanding that true inner responsiveness depends on our capacity not to react immediately when someone has finished speaking, but to give ourselves time to fully *heed* what has been said and give it a second, more inward hearing. The therapist's inner hearing can in turn generate a type of inner sight or 'in-sight', but only if their gaze is an inner listening gaze, not one directed at the body or eyes of the client. Silent and sustained eye-contact with a client can indeed be a most powerful medium of core contact and communication, yet this is not always appropriate to the therapeutic relationship. For just as eye-contact is most powerful when it is silent, not accompanied by speaking, so is 'ear contact' most powerful when it is not accompanied by looking. One of the biggest obstacles for therapists in learning how to listen maieutically is the habit of looking at a client whilst listening to them, whether or not the latter meets the therapist's gaze. This turns the client into a specular object, whilst at the same time preventing the therapist from turning their own gaze inward and learning to contact and *hold* the client in the *inner gaze of their listening intent*. Only through *withholding* and *holding* the client in their inner gaze can the therapist's inner listening become a type of inner sight - one through which they not only hear but *behold* the client in a new way.

Inner Hearing and Inner Seeing

'Thinking is a listening which brings something to view…something one can hear. In doing so it brings into view what was unheard (of).'

Martin Heidegger

The practice of maieutic listening prepares the ground for a special type of intuitive perception or in-sight. Its basis is the listener's ability to turn their gaze inwards, withdrawing energy from their bodily eyes and peering into the darkness within their souls, *as if* they had their eyes closed. By not focusing visually on the client's body or face, the therapist can listen more effectively with their own body, hearkening to the silence beneath their words and sensing in a quite physical way the relationship between an individual's speaking body and personality and the silent inner core of their being. The in-sight that the listener then develops is not like the physical perception of an object but is a feeling perception of this fundamental *relationship*. If, at the same time, the therapist is also able to let images arise of the *objective* situations, events and relationships that the client describes, it becomes possible for them to enter and dwell within these images as within a dream. The maieutic listener 'sleeps' into the speech of the other, not only in order to share the person's experience of the event or relationship, but in order to feel it from the perspective of their sleeping inner being. The type of perception that then develops can be compared to the unborn child's experience, from within the womb, of events experienced by the mother during pregnancy. The extent to which an individual is able to stay in tune and in touch with their inner being in their everyday life and relationships is comparable to the mother's ability to stay in touch with her baby during pregnancy. Just as the baby in the womb is invisible and inaudible to physical perception so is the client's inner being. The midwife must come close to the mother's belly to hearken to the baby within, or use ultrasound scans to see it. But the maieutic listener can develop an inner picture of an individual's relationship to this being by (a) listening closely to the way the person speaks about themselves whilst at the same time hearkening to the being that speaks through their words, and (b) by attending closely to the verbal picture they give of different events and relationships, whilst at the same time feeling their way into these pictures. This feeling in-sight will in turn generate intellectual insights. These do not take the form of borrowed psychoanalytic metaphors such as those used to 'interpret' dreams, but of metaphorical images - images which, like those of our dreams themselves, require no interpretation, for they are precise interpretations of directly *felt* comprehensions.

Maieutic Listening and 'Transference'

Maieutic listening is an attunement to what Buber called the 'interhuman' dimension of meaning, the open and inexhaustible realm of *shared* human questions - 'we' questions - which each individual experiences in their own personal way, as 'I' questions. Many therapists, on the other hand, are concerned to separate their own process from that of the client. Because of this, there is a constant need to translate what goes on between therapist and client into something going on 'in' them or in the client, to translate 'we' questions into 'I' or 'you' questions, 'we' feelings into 'I' or 'you' feelings. Unexpected and unfamiliar 'I' feelings experienced by the therapist need then to be explained as transferred 'you' feelings belonging to the client - as the client's rage or sadness, not mine. The practical need for these concepts of transference and counter-transference comes from seeing feelings as the *private property* of the personal self, as internal objects which can be owned or disowned, exchanged or transferred. This view makes it difficult for the therapist to hear and acknowledge echoes of their 'own' feelings and questions in those of the client. But without hearing these echoes they cannot acknowledge the meaning that their own way of relating to these shared issues might hold for the client - and vice versa. Whenever a significant relationship is formed between two people, it is because they embody and express certain unborn aspects and potentials of each other's being. This is where the meaning of human relationships lies. The meanings we communicate in speech are expressions of what we *mean* to one another in this deeper sense - a meaning that has to do essentially with what we *are* for one another, the aspects of ourselves we find embodied and expressed in others. Quite independently of any processes of 'transference' or 'counter-transference', therefore, the personality and character of the therapist will mean something to the client and vice versa. Understanding this makes it impossible to separate listening and being; *how* a therapist listens from who they are and how they embody and express their being. A therapist may be aware of familiar experiences, feelings, issues or aspects of themselves 'reflected' in the client, and as a result feel either more or less comfortable in working with them. Maieutic listening, on the other hand, not only requires an awareness on the part of the therapist of the familiar or unfamiliar aspects of themselves embodied by a client. It also requires an awareness of how, as an individual, the therapist may also embody significant unborn aspects of the client. In this way maieutic listening is itself the embodiment of a fundamental principle of human 'inter-being' - the fact that we are each parts of one another and embody aspects of each other's being. This is of particular significance in communication, for it implies that in a quite general and fundamental sense we speak *for* each other - not just for ourselves or *to* each other. Or rather, we speak for each other's *other* selves, each other's latent and unborn aspects or potentialities of being. Empathic understanding on the other hand, is limited by those aspects of ourselves we are already familiar with - excluding those other selves we embody and express for each other. This is another way in which maieutic listening is quite distinct from 'empathic listening'. Its significance lies in the fact that the health not only of the 'therapeutic relationship' but of all dyadic human relationships rests ultimately on each partner's capacity to acknowledge both the aspects of themselves embodied and expressed by others and the aspects of others they themselves embody and express for them.

Closeness and Distance

Usually it is only through separation or distance that each partner begins to acknowledge aspects of the other as aspects of themselves. The therapist's attempt to balance personal involvement and intimacy, on the one hand, with professional distance and restraint on the other, conceals a third dimension of the therapeutic relationship. This is an intimacy achieved *through* personal distance, in which both therapist and client begin to work with each other internally, as aspects of themselves. This personal distance is what allows true professional closeness to the client. In any dyadic relationship, it is often only in relationships outside the dyad that people feel able to embody and express those aspects of themselves previously associated with their partner. All this applies to the therapeutic relationship also, invariably giving rise to a set of parallelisms or 'synchronicities' between the therapist's relationships and experience outside of therapy and those of the client. It is through awareness of these parallelisms that the therapist begins to understand not only what the client's experience means to them but also what their experience means to the client. Then the therapist can not only respond verbally to the client with helpful insights drawn from their experience but communicate on a silent and core level from who they are - consciously embodying aspects of themselves they know to be of significance for the client and in the client's relationships. This embodied communication is a basic dimension of the maieutic listener's bodywork.

Energy and Meaning

The aim of maieutic listening is to bridge the gap between talking and touching therapies, analysis and bodywork, i.e. between therapies focused on *meaning* and those focused on *energy*. Perhaps the most important link between them lies in what it means to question something. A question that a therapist puts to the client verbally, but does not themselves *experience* as a question, is a meaningless question, devoid of energetic charge. A question the therapist experiences within themselves is an energetically charged question. Such a question will communicate, whether it is put into words or not. But the therapist may easily be tempted by their professional role to put verbal questions to the client in order precisely to avoid experiencing their charge. Every verbal question is also an implicit statement, an anticipation of the type of answer expected or wanted. Questions that the listener communicates silently and wordlessly, by allowing their charge to build up, always bring their own answer up but one free of the preconceptions that the worded questions inevitably carry.

We use language to represent the relationships between things and between people. We have questions because we cannot mentally represent a relationship. When a question has emotional charge, it is because we experience the absent relationship as a tension or potential energy - like the potential energy created by two electrically charged plates between which no current is flowing. In therapy, one basic way in which meaning is experienced is through the potential energy of an experienced question, experienced as a bodily charge or tension. Another aspect of meaning is the energetic flow that can result from this tension or charge, but only if it is (a) allowed to build up, and (b) not abruptly short-circuited and *discharged*. When the therapist uses words to 'make connections' or asks the client to do so, the crucial question is whether or not the potential energy and deeper meaning of the question has been allowed to build up, and whether or not the connection is intended merely to discharge whatever energy has accumulated, and pre-empt its deeper meaning. The basic discipline of maieutic listening - that of withholding the spoken word - does not imply a rigid posture of mute silence on the part of the therapist. Its aim is to ensure that no questions are put or connections made through language, without the therapist first allowing the energy and meaning of the question to be experienced on a deeper level - in a wordless and bodily way. Withholding is the capacity to hold the charge of an experienced question, and to avoid its pre-emptive discharge. The therapist's capacity for maieutic listening is their *capacitance*. Capacitance is the therapist's capacity to 'bear with' the client as a listener i.e. bearing the tension of the question with the client, acknowledging it as a shared question, and a shared tension. Withholding prevents the therapist seeking relief from this tension through answers verbally elicited from the client or offered verbally to them.

A Question of Being

Existential psychotherapy has long recognised that behind the personal questions that people bring to therapy are certain fundamental and shared questions of human beings, questions to do with life and death, choice and responsibility, aloneness and relatedness. These are questions traditionally addressed by philosophy rather than psychology. The courage of Heidegger and Buber lay in recognising that fundamental philosophical questions, like those of psychotherapy have to do with our relationship *to* things and *to* people, and not merely with our scientific view of the relationships that exist *between* them. It was Heidegger who recognised that for philosophy to go further in exploring the meaning of being and of meaning, it must be rooted in a deeper way of listening and relating *to* Being. It was Buber who recognised that this also involves searching for a deeper way of listening and relating to individual *beings*. Behind every significant question is the pain of an experienced distance from our own being and from other beings, a distance which can, paradoxically, bring us closer to them. Maieutic listening understands all human questions as expressions of a fundamental quest - the quest to relate to our own being and to other beings. It is this quest which forms the basis of the 'will to meaning'. But like feeling, meaning is not just something we discover but something we do. Authentic listening, like authentic speech, is about meaning another human being, not just as a person but as a being.

Core Relatedness and Spiritual Intimacy

The human being is the human embodiment of their inner being. This inner being is not itself anything human. Nor, however, is it inhuman, for it is the source of all the human feelings and qualities we are capable of bodying and embodying. But the failure to distinguish the human body and the human being, the personal 'I' and the inner Thou, is the source of man's inhumanity to man, for behind the abuse of persons lies a desperate quest for a sense of spiritual intimacy - a sense of core relatedness to other beings. The intense charge of this quest is not experienced as such but acted out and discharged by stripping others of their humanity, murdering their bodies or abusing the person. The problem raised at the beginning of this article, namely that ours is a culture which knows only two modes of intimacy, physical and emotional, sexual and personal, touchy and feely, but lacks any sense of what it means to make core contact - spiritual contact - with another being cannot be underestimated.

Whereas Freud challenged the sexual taboos of his day, maieutic listening challenges spiritual taboos - the taboo on experiencing and cultivating spiritual intimacy, intercourse and procreation. Each day we are given the chance to meet and be met by others, touch and be touched by them, seed and be seeded by them. Or at least we would be if we didn't wear spiritual contraceptives, if we were more capable of bearing the pregnancies that result, and less prone to seek to abort, mentally or emotionally, the new aspects of ourselves that have been fertilised. Pregnancy is not an illness, but disease is a type of spiritual pregnancy or miscarriage. The purpose of therapy is not to help others abort or evacuate, repress or release what they carry pregnantly within them, but to help them in the work of bodying it, and in *this* way giving birth to it. The role of the listener is one of midwife - being with, bearing with and showing what it means to hold the emotional charge of this pregnancy and go through the labour of birth without forcing delivery. The essential 'work' of *maieutic* listening is itself a form of inner 'bodywork' - the capacity to inwardly bear and body the charge of a felt question - whether formulated or still unformulated. Its aim is to meet another human being through the embodied presence of our own being. Its value for the bodyworker does not lie in helping them to 'be somebody', to successfully conform to their professional role and its accompanying status and self-image, but rather to *body their being*. This means to 'be a body' and not just an empathic 'mind'. Only through the embodied presence and bodily receptivity of the listener can listening itself be experienced as a form of resonant inner contact and communication between human beings.

Nothing will work of whatever works they work,
who are not great in Being.

Meister Eckhart

How far is the truth susceptible of embodiment?
That is the question. That is the experiment.

Nietzsche

MAIEUTIC LISTENING AND ANALYSIS

Towards a Fundamental Rethinking
of Psychotherapy Training

Introduction

It is almost universally accepted that the role of a counsellor or therapist is not to answer a client's questions or solve their problems, give them advice or impose interpretations on what they say. And yet many counsellors and therapists, particularly - but not only - those lacking experience or still in training, regard their listening merely as (a) a way of giving clients opportunity to speak and (b) a prelude to offering some form of (hopefully) helpful verbal response. Indeed it is by the quality, appropriacy and therapeutic efficacy of their words and body language that a therapist's skills are principally judged. Too often this leads the therapist either into a pre-occupation with finding the right thing to say, to reliance on pre-established patterns of response (mirroring, paraphrase, elicitative questioning etc.) or to the use of pre-rehearsed prompts and therapeutic techniques.

Much of the fault for this situation lies with the nature of the training given to counsellors, therapists and analysts. This usually includes reading and theoretical seminars, case discussions, personal therapy and supervision. In addition, practice may be provided, through role play and other methods, in specific therapeutic techniques. This diversity of approach conceals an enormous lacuna. For though it is the depth, tone and style of the therapist's listening that will primarily colour and determine the course of the therapy (for both client and therapist) there exists as yet no form of psychotherapeutic training in which the nature and development of the trainee's listening is taken as the primary concern. This apparent abnormality reflects the norms of our social culture, which treats speech and action as the most direct forms of communication and sees listening merely as a *passive* or *preparatory* phase of verbal or physical expression.

I believe that a deeper phenomenology of listening would understand speech and body language, words and deeds, as indirect verbal and physical forms of communication, and acknowledge listening itself as a *direct form of non-verbal and non-physical communication*. From this point of view listening is never a mere prelude to verbal or physical response. It is itself a form of direct inner response. The way we hear what someone says, says something to them. The way we understand their words communicates wordlessly. Our way of listening, in and of itself, carries back (relates) something to the speaker. In a most fundamental sense, listening *is* relating - our way of *being* with another human being, of being *with* that human being and of responding to what goes on between ourselves and another.

Authentic listening is an attunement to what Martin Buber called 'the between' or 'the interhuman' (*das Zwischenmenschliche*), an open and inexhaustible domain of *shared* human questions, values and challenges (so-called 'we-meanings') which each individual translates into their own unique language of being ('I-meanings'). Many therapists, on the other hand, see themselves as needing to separate their own feelings and questions from those of the client. They seek to translate what goes on *between* them and their clients into something going on 'in' them or 'in' the client, translating 'we-meanings' into 'I' or 'you-meanings' and in this way treating experience as private property. As a result they are then surprised or disturbed to hear a 'synchronistic' echo of their 'own' feelings, failings and challenges in the emotional life of a client. Rather than understanding this synchronicity in terms of underlying 'we-meanings', they are fearful of 'counter-transference' (of translating 'I-meanings' into 'you-meanings'). Yet every dialogue is in essence a *co-respondence* of both parties to a third voice - the voice of 'the between' or 'We'. If the therapist's listening is a response to the between, it will in itself call forth a co-response from the client. Verbal responses, on the other hand, tend to impose a structure of 'I-meanings' and 'you-meanings'.

The basic discipline of maieutic listening is the withholding of verbal response, not just in the form of interruptions, advice or pre-emptive interpretations but even in the form of verbal questions and promptings. This does not mean that the maieutic listener never interrupts, questions or puts verbal suggestions to a client. But training in maieutic listening concentrates on our capacity to *be with* others in silence, to question silently rather than in words, to hold and touch others with our listening gaze and to maintain our listening attunement to 'the between'. Being-in-silence with another means finding a way of presencing and embodying our own being - of 'being-a-body' - that does not rely on words, gestures or on the acting out of a role. For too many therapists, however, it is precisely their role as therapists that allows them to 'be some-body'. Their training concentrates on perfecting this role rather than on learning to 'be there' in an embodied way; on listening and communicating 'in role' rather than through their *embodied presence*. Methods of training have not been sought or found by which to cultivate the trainee's capacity for authentic listening - for 'being with', 'being in silence' and 'being a body'. Instead the resources of scientific, psychoanalytic, and even phenomenological thinking have been entirely focused on the client and his or her psychopathology, and not on the *listening praxis of the therapist*. A listening psychology should, by contrast, explore the nature and therapeutic dimensions of listening itself, and put the spotlight of psychotherapy training firmly on the therapist *as* listener.

Questions to do with the nature of psychotherapeutic listening and its significance in psychotherapy training are by no means merely questions of concern to the professional. They have to do with the underlying social pathology of our culture - a rift between language and being. This rift can be described in many ways - as a rift between reflective and pre-reflective awareness, words and wordless cognition, the ego and the inner self. I describe it as a split between the speaking self and the listening self, the language mind and the listening body. The aim of therapeutic listening is not simply to let the client speak but to nurture 'authentic speech'. That is why the therapist's own style and depth of listening is so important to the client. Authentic speech is a *listening speech*, responsive to our wordless, bodily and felt sense of meaning. The object of the therapist's listening is not simply to respond in a helpful way to the client's speech but to help the client to *listen to themselves* in a deeper way. The primary aim of the therapist is therefore to model and embody this deeper way of listening to oneself. 'Not knowing how to listen, neither can they speak.' (Heraclitus). It needs to be firmly understood that the *essential* focus of therapeutic listening is not the client's *speech* at all, but rather the client's own way of listening or not listening to themselves in the process of *coming to speak*.

Before listening can take up the central place it should be expected to have in all forms of counselling and psychotherapy training, what is needed is deep, phenomenological exploration of the nature of listening as such. What is also called for is a phenomenological language of listening freed of all the current terminological frameworks of psychotherapy and psychoanalysis. In the course of my own work I have defined and refined a basic phenomenological language of listening condensed into a dozen or so guiding words or 'keywords'. These guiding words are derived principally, but not exclusively, from the thinking of Martin Heidegger and Donald Winnicott. They include words such as 'hearkening' and 'heeding', 'holding' and 'withholding', 'hosting' and 'hallowing'. These are not technical terms or abstract concepts. Nor are they merely suggestive invocations. They articulate dimensions of a highly specific listening praxis and of a particular and profound experience of listening which I call, for historical, philosophical and metaphorical reasons, 'maieusis'. This is an experience of listening as 'inner voice communication', a term which I coined in an informal experimental and experiential circle that has been ongoing since 1975 and in which we created and explored a non-verbal pair exercise bearing this name. 'Inner voice communication' is one of the foundation exercises in maieutic listening. Its essential discipline is the discipline referred to by Heidegger as the central discipline of thinking itself - a patient restraint or 'withholding' (*Verhaltenheit*) of the naming word that allows us to persevere in a silent, inner questioning.

'Patience is the truly human way of being.' (Heidegger). The distinction between *homo sapiens* and *homo patiens*, man as a knowing being and man as a patient 'suffering' being, has been expressed in many different ways in human culture. Modern psychiatry formalises this distinction as a social role division between the trained and qualified 'expert' in possession of medical-pharmaceutical knowledge and the suffering but medically ignorant 'patient'. But it is not only medicine and psychiatry that are tainted by the dichotomy. The spheres of counselling, psychotherapy and psychoanalysis can also fall prey to a tacit belief in the superior knowing and greater mental 'health' of the professional practitioner, on the one hand, and, on the other hand, whatever cognitive-emotional-behavioural or neuro-chemical deficiencies are attributed to the client. It is as if the psychotherapist is assumed, simply by virtue of their professional position, to be able to feel (*pathein*) and respond to the essential suffering (*pathos*) of a client without themselves 'suffering'. Even more dangerously, psychotherapy can come to tacitly share the implicit assumption of medical-model psychiatry that 'abnormal' depths and intensities of feeling are intrinsically 'pathological'. Instead of acknowledging the deep human *pathos* of the client's situation, it is seen as a pathology to be 'treated'. The pathologisation of suffering is central to the commercially and medically-promoted health paranoia of our culture - a culture which fetishises an idealised concept of 'wellness' or 'well-being'.

The word 'client' derives from the Latin *cluere* - 'to be called'. Whilst it is accepted that therapists need themselves to be *patient* listeners in order to respond to the call of their clients' suffering, current models of counselling and psychotherapy do not explore in any fundamental way the inner relation between *pathos* and so-called 'psychopathology'. In a culture more and more dominated by an ethos of 'positive thinking' we no longer have patience with suffering of any sort. It is as if the patiently suffered contractions and labour of childbirth were seen *only* as a source of 'unnecessary' pain and suffering and not also of great joy, wonder and even bodily pleasure.

Whenever we find our state of being 'unbearable' we pay homage to a wisdom buried and yet still pregnant in language itself. The English verb 'to bear' has the double meaning of to carry or withstand ('to bear a burden') and to give birth ('she bore a child'). In our technological age, pregnancy is often regarded as a dangerous and quasi-pathological condition to be treated and 'managed' like an illness. Medical science does not even consider the opposite viewpoint - that instead of pregnancy being a form of illness, all illness may essentially be a form of pregnancy - no less potentially painful but also no less meaningful and fruitful. As far as psychotherapy is concerned however, the medical model of illness and the medical pathologisation of the patient renders us incapable of cultivating a way of listening which is 'maieutic' - one in which the listener understands themselves as *patient midwife* to a rebirth of the client's own self.

The basic pathology of our age is not aids or cancer, neurosis or schizophrenia. It is the incapacity to listen 'maieutically' - to be and bear with ourselves and others in pregnant silence. Yet if silence are suffering are to bear fruit they must first be felt and borne in silence. If psychotherapeutic listening is to bear fruit, the inner bearing of the therapist must be that of patient midwife. The true midwife however, is not someone who relies on their professional knowledge, training or skills alone but someone whose whole embodied presence creates a larger womb - a sheltering or 'holding' environment. The midwife is someone able to quite literally be and bear with others in pregnant silence, and someone whose whole way of handling others is imbued with a hallowing reverence for that which seeks to bear itself forth and come to birth.

To be a midwife demands *character*. Today however, the whole focus of our culture is on the person and personality. Psychiatrists speak of 'personality disorders' of different types. Holistic health practitioners speak of treating 'the whole person'. Counsellors are 'person-centred'. The philosophy of maieutic listening on the other hand, offers us an entirely new understanding not only of 'personality' but also of 'character' - and of their essential difference. What we call 'personality' is the everyday way in which we bear ourselves forth in the world. *Per-sonare* means to 'sound forth'. The word *persona* referred to the facial masks worn by actors in the past - masks which were both the face they presented to the audience and the medium through which (*per-*) their voices sounded (*sonare*). Personality is the outward way in which we personify or impersonate ourselves in speech and gesture. Character, on the other hand, is more a matter of how we comport or bear ourselves in silence - our inner bearing or comportment.

The essential *genealogy* of character is connected with the way we each come to speech from silence - with the 'coming to be' (*genesis*) of the word (*logos*). The way we come to ourselves 'through the word' (*dia-logos*) depends on the way we ourselves come to words, i.e.: the way we listen to ourselves before we speak. To think before we speak is to listen before we speak, for thinking itself is the process of translating what our listening awareness brings to light.

The Principles and Praxis of Maieutic Listening

No subject is more marginalized in the psychotherapeutic literature than the art of listening - even though it is central to the practice of both medicine and psychotherapy. Listening is seen as a mere prelude to verbal response, diagnosis or interpretation, or reduced to a set of technical-professional skills. No profession is more marginalized than that of the midwife - she who brings life into the world - for in our culture medical technology seeks to dispense with her art. 'Maieutic' listening is a therapeutic listening praxis based specifically on the inner bearing or comportment of the midwife (Greek *maieuesthai* - to act as a midwife). Listening as *maieusis* is inherently therapeutic, for it is about helping others to *bear with* their own feelings in a fruitful way and in this way transform their suffering into the birthpangs of a new inner bearing towards the world and other people - one that helps them to once again 'find their bearings' in the world. The client being essentially pregnant with a new way of being-in-the-world, the maieutic listener must themselves adopt an inner bearing attuned to that pregnant state of being, and be the very model of a midwife - someone able to be and bear with others in their suffering.

When a woman is pregnant, she needs to adjust her physical posture and comportment in order to accommodate her big belly and her lowered centre of gravity. To engage in maieutic listening is to lower the centre of gravity of our listening to the belly region. To listen not with the head or heart alone - a typically Western bearing - but with what in Japan is called 'hara'. One meaning of *hara* is 'belly talk'. This is an expression which shows a deep understanding of listening as a mode of silent communication issuing from the belly region. *Hara* is the site of what the Greek thinker Heraclitus called *logos* -

the wordless inner resonance or reverberation of the psyche, echoing not in words but in tones of silence - feeling tones.

Feeling tones are not emotions but the basic wavelengths of being through which we attune to others and sound them out in our listening. The listener does not only attend to the speaker's voice and feeling tones. The listener also sets a tone. The tone of our listening is picked up by others even before they begin to speak, influencing what and how they communicate to us. Listening with *hara* means attuning to the essential or fundamental tone of our being. This enables us to 'sound out' the other with our whole being and not just with our head or heart; to inwardly lean or 'list' with our whole being towards the being of the other i.e. to *list-en*.

The pregnant mother is connected with her baby through the umbilical cord. When the umbilical cord is cut at birth, the baby's physical connection with the womb is severed. Its 'being-in-the-womb' becomes a 'being-in-the-world' and then, as it acquires its mother tongue, a 'being-in-the-word'. As adults we use words to ask each other questions, draw each other out, and sound out each other's thoughts and feelings. Western culture understands communication as either verbal or physical. Japanese culture, on the other hand, retained for a long time the awareness of a type of human intercourse and intimacy dependent neither on sounds and words nor on physical contact and touch, but on the touch of what I call the 'listening body'. This can be compared to an invisible psychic womb or capsule that remains after birth and that is sensed by both man and woman whenever they experience 'gut feelings' in the belly. This womb is filled not with the waters of the amniotic sac but with the equally fluid medium of feeling tone.

The words *tone, tense, tension, tend, tent, attend, intend* etc all have a common root meaning - 'stretching' or 'spanning'. As the pregnant mother's belly expands inwardly, her skin surface expands and becomes taut. Maieutic listening, as an attunement to pregnant silence, also involves an inward expansion of the 'womb' of our own listening body - not the belly itself but its psychic interiority or soul-space. The *intent* to inwardly expand our soul-womb or soul-belly - the inner soul-space of our listening - goes hand in hand with a deepened abdominal breathing and also slight muscular tensioning of the abdomen that I call 'in-tensioning'.

The umbilical cord reaches inside the womb to the body of the foetus. In reaching inside our own listening body to contact our listening self we inwardly extend an umbilical cord to a still-point of silence within our belly or uterus. This is what I call 'in-tending'. The still-point of silence lies in the lower abdomen or *hara*. This is not just a centre of awareness in ourselves but a centre linking us to our innermost being and that of others. This is a being we never cease to bear within us, a being that is forever unborn and in this sense 'pregnant' within us, but is also the source of all those *potentials of being* we seek constantly to give birth to. When we really make inner contact with others in our listening, it feels as if there is an invisible fibre or 'tendril of intent' *inwardly extending* from our centre of awareness in the *hara* and connecting us umbilically with its counterpart in the 'belly' or 'soul womb' of the other. With this tendril of intent we can touch the innermost being or 'core self' of the other with and from our own innermost being or core self - our listening self. Whenever such 'core contact' with another is established umbilically from the *hara,* it endures. For whatever the physical distance between two people they remain inwardly connected through the tendril or umbilicus. There are 'silver threads of silence' connecting us inwardly with all those with whom we share a deep inner connection, constantly available to keep us 'in contact' and 'in touch' with them - and doing so without the help of mobile phones.

Just as our nearness or distance of our inner listening contact with others cannot be measured in terms of physical space, nor can the listening *time* that we grant to others. Deep listening does not require time. It *grants* time, inwardly expanding the psychological *time-space* in which we connect with others. This time-space can be compared to the time-space experienced by the foetus in the womb - a spacious present that is not yet divided into past, present and future. Maieutic listening is the inward expansion of the womb of the moment and of the psychological time-space it encompasses.

Listening does not mean simply giving another person our whole hearted outward 'attention' - hanging on their every word and being sensitive to their every gesture, intonation and facial expression. It means opening an inner time-space within ourselves in which to take them into the very womb of our souls. For this, no amount of outer attention to others suffices without the simultaneous *intent* to listen inwardly to ourselves. For unless we listen inwardly to our own core self, we cannot listen to another with the inner ear of that self, nor make inner contact with others from that self. Maieutic listening is an intense listening that requires the most concentrated 'in-tending' of our awareness - the most concentrated *intention* as well as *attention.* We attend to 'some-thing' - an audible remark or visible gesture. We intend some-one - a being. Maieutic listening is listening with intent - a listening that *intends* a contact with own inner being and that of the other, and in this way establishes inner contact between them.

Such listening with intent is by no means the same thing as having some sort of calculative purpose or agenda, listening *for* some-thing, or *in order* to do or get some-thing. Intending to listen deeply does not mean listening with ulterior intent. Intentful listening is a most direct form of *relating* which carries or bears back (*re-lates*) the inner bearing and perceptions of the listener. It creates a telepathic carrier wave of attunement on which rich messages can ride. If listening were simply a matter of *attention* we could reduce it to a skill or technique. It would make no difference *who* was listening and *who* was being listened to, as long as the 'right' sort of attention was given. But the 'who' does make a difference. In listening with our whole being we also *communicate* our whole being. Who we *are* 'speaks'. The phrase 'I *hear* you' then means 'I hear *you*' - not sound vibrations or words, nor even meanings and feelings. But for me to say 'I hear *you*' it must be the case that '*I* hear you' - that I am there with my whole being.

'*We* hear, not the ear.' Heidegger

Like the foetus in the womb, the inner being of an individual is not something visible or audible. The contact we establish with another being is not a physical contact. When we really make contact with someone through our eyes, for example, it is not because we are staring at or studying their eyes optically. As soon as we focus our vision on someone's eyes as physical objects we break any inner contact established through our *gaze*. In the gaze '*I* see, not the eye' and I see *you*, not your eyes. The same is true of listening. And just as we can hold someone in our visual gaze so we can also hold someone in our aural gaze, our inner listening gaze. This is the inner gaze of our listening intent, centred not in the eyes or ears, the head or heart, but in the *hara*.

In Western culture we are familiar with the experience of genuine eye-contact, touching another with our gaze or being touched by the gaze of the other. We are not so familiar with the experience of touching another with our inner listening gaze or being so touched. Yet just as we can feel someone's gaze in a tangible and almost tactile way, even if we are not facing them, so we can feel touched by their listening gaze. In Western culture we know also the experience of the *mutual* gaze and the rich inner communication that can take place through it. We know the mutual gaze through the experience of the mutual visual gaze, however, and not as 'belly talk' - the silent inner communication and communion of listeners. We make communicative contact principally by looking at people and speaking to them, and not by listening to them. Yet just as we can make contact with someone in our visual gaze, so too can we make contact with our inner listening gaze. Indeed if we do not, there will be no real contact at all - however many words, gestures and looks are exchanged. And just as we can seek to hold someone in our visual gaze, so we can also hold another person in our inner listening gaze.

We hear sounds. But we hearken to silence. One dimension of maieutic listening is hearkening to that still-point of silence in the abdomen or *hara* through which we establish inner listening contact with others. Another dimension of maieutic listening is *holding* - sustaining this inner listening contact with our own inner being and that of the other over a period of time. 'Holding' here, means the other in the inner gaze of our listening intent.

Neither *hearkening* nor *holding* require that we be looking at someone as they speak i.e., attending to them visually. For they are not forms of listening attention, but of listening intention. This intention is also a type of inner tonation or 'intonation' of our listening. When we establish inner listening contact with another person, the inner *tone* of our listening is something that communicates directly and without words. The way we hear what they say says something to them. The way we understand their words communicates wordlessly. The medium of this inner communication is the inner tone of our listening. Learning to modulate this is a third dimension of maieutic listening, one that I call 'handling', for the tone of our listening is a vibration that touches the other even before they begin to speak. What a person says to us and the way they say it is already a response to the sensed inner tone of our listening - the wavelength on which we are open to 'hearing' them. This wavelength is also vibration that touches the other directly, setting a tone for what they will say and the way they will say it.

In everyday language, when we speak of 'handling people sensitively' we mean either speaking to them or touching them in a sensitive way. Learning to listen maieutically means learning not only to *hearken* to or *hold* others in the inner gaze of our listening intent but also to *handle* them sensitively through the inner tone and touch of our listening intent. *Handling* another with our listening intent means being able to subtly modulate its inner tone and pressure of touch.

Just as our perception of someone is invariably echoed in the voice tone with which we respond to them, so does our listening carry its own silent intonation. Even without responding to someone vocally, our feelings communicate as tones of silence. Indeed it is these tones of silence - these listening tones - that are echoed and translated into tones of voice and the tone of our words. Language and vocal communication are translations of an 'inner voice communication' that we only experience directly through the silent tones of our own or other people's listening. In listening to her baby, the pregnant mother communicates to her baby. So too can the midwife. Not with her speaking self but with her listening self, her 'foetal self'. Not with her physical body but with her own listening body, her 'womb body'. The listening body is the body *as* womb, as the place in which feelings incubate and the site of our inner, felt sense of meaning. Listening as *maieusis* is an 'inner voice communication' between the listening self and listening body of the hearer and that of the speaker, like a communication between two babies in the same joint womb. This joint womb or 'bi-personal field' created in maieutic listening connects the listening bodies of two people. Handling people by 'sensitively' adjusting our language and tone of voice compensates to a certain degree for handling them through the silent tone and touch of our listening. The avoidance of silence in conversation is an attempt to avoid the intimacy of the bi-personal field - of inner touch, *holding* and *handling*. Handling also has to do with the way the listener influences and modulates the length and depth of conversational silences. By restraining our speaking selves from immediate verbal or physical responses to another person's words we draw down the gravitational centre of their listening, enabling them to dwell deeper in their own inner silence and become aware of the silent communication going on in 'the between'. Withholding does not mean simply delaying our response - holding back our feelings or questions. It means learning to let these feelings and questions mature within us - to *harbour* them as silent feelings and silent questions.

Withholding is not just saying nothing: not-speaking. It is an active form of 'unspeaking' - for in choosing to listen we also choose to leave what we might have said unspoken. What is *un*spoken by the listener is also un*spoken* - left on 'the table of silence' - for the speaker to become aware of and 'pick up'. If we think or feel something as we listen but do not say it, we need not be surprised if another person 'picks it up' and articulates it.

To express something in words does not mean to reveal it - for words can just as much conceal and cover up as reveal. Similarly, to leave something unspoken - to 'withhold' verbal expression of a thought, feeling, or question does not necessarily mean to conceal it in silence. 'Withholding' is also 'with-holding' or 'holding with' - *holding* an unspoken thought, feeling or question *with* the other until they themselves feel safe in *handling* it in their own way - 'picking up on it', 'picking it up' for themselves and expressing it in their own terms.

If we use 'with-holding' to harbour a question in silence, we should not be surprised to find it directly or indirectly sensed and answered by the speaker. Yet to maintain an ongoing verbal dialogue with clients, some therapists are still tempted to use questions to fill what they experience as uncomfortably long gaps of silence. On one level, this is a perfectly understandable and professional procedure. It is, after all important to get a clear picture of the individual's thoughts and feelings, their life-world and relationships. On another level, however, such questioning can easily come in the way of a deeper listening.

It is part of the basic protocol of therapy that the therapist should not seek to play God by providing the client with *answers* to their emotional or existential questions. The purpose of this protocol is clear - to help clients to feel their questions, formulate them for themselves and find their own answers within themselves.

Paradoxically, however, the same professional protocol of 'not answering questions' is not applied to the therapist's questions. Unlike the client, the therapist is instead free at any time to put their *own* questions to the client and thereby make the client responsible for answering them. This freedom prevents the therapist from taking the same degree of responsibility that is demanded of the client - the responsibility to feel out and find answers to their questions within themselves. This requires the disciplines of withholding interrogative questioning and its counterpart - an ability on the part of the therapist to *harbour* their own questions in pregnant silence.

It is only by *harbouring* their own questions that therapists are able to (1) responsibly *own* these questions as *their* questions as well as questions relevant to the client, (2) feel for answers to them in themselves instead of seeking answers only from the client (3) avoid framing the questions in words that may predispose the client to a certain type of answer, and (4) give the client time to feel, formulate and find answers to the questions themselves.

Maieutic listening involves *hearkening* for the implicit or unstated questions hinted at by a client's words - not as a prelude to immediately articulating these questions for the client, but in order for the therapist to *heed* these questions, take them to heart as shared questions, to consciously *harbour* them in silence, and in this way also to hold them open. Questions which a therapist consciously *harbours* and *holds open* in this way have a vivid and tangible reality in 'the between' - they stand out clearly on the table of silence, but in a way that does not predispose or foreclose the client's own response. Holding questions open should not be confused with asking 'open questions'. The term 'holding open' refers to the inner bearing of the listener, not some modality of verbal response. This inner bearing is one of *reverence for the mystery at the core of every question.*

The closer a therapist gets to the 'core' of a client's issues, the more the questions that are raised take the form of fundamental 'spiritual' questions of life and death, freedom and responsibility, aloneness and togetherness, meaning and value fulfilment that are *common* to all human beings. Only by *harbouring* a felt question in pregnant silence do we allow sufficient time for a truly fitting formulation of the question to gestate or incubate itself within us. In this way we prevent ourselves from prematurely giving birth to the questions - framing it in an off-hand way that forecloses all deeper questions and forces a superficial answer. Only by inwardly *holding open* a space in which to *harbour* a question in pregnant silence before framing it in words do we open ourselves to the mystery at its core - the deeper felt questions that are seeking to formulate themselves within us.

A genuinely listening *dialogue* is not a Socratic to-and-fro of Question and Answer but a wordless *questing* - one that does not use verbal questions to frame and foreclose in advance the felt but as yet unformulated questions that weigh upon us. Listening dialogue happens because when we allow ourselves to harbour and hold open a felt question within us, we are already inviting an answer, one that will come to us as soon as the true question finds its formulation - and do so without the forceps of confessional interrogation.

In *harbouring* a question we give both ourselves and others an opportunity to fully feel the question - indeed to *be* the question. *Being* the question allows us to *become* the answer. 'Becoming' the answer means finding a felt question answered through a felt shift in our very sense of self - of who we are. With this birth of a new sense of self comes the birth of a new inner bearing towards other people and the world. We do not seek answers to questions in order to find ways of changing ourselves. We find ourselves changed by bearing our own felt questions - changed in a way that *is* the answer.

Whenever we use language to prematurely grasp for answers to felt questions it is like grasping objects that rest on 'the table of silence' to brandish as 'insights' or 'interpretations'. This can leave the table emptied, the silence bare, the questions foreclosed and unavailable for others to pick up, handle and *feel*. Meaning then evaporates. Truly deep therapeutic questions and answers, insights and interpretations, on the other hand, always and only arise from *harbouring* and *holding open* felt questions.

Maieutic listening, with its central discipline of withholding, does not imply abstinence from speech but cultivates deep *listening dialogue* and deep *listening speech*. Listening speech is a *hinting* speech, using language not to *grasp* objects from the table of silence but rather to point another to them. Listening dialogue takes the form of *hinting* because it uses language to communicate 'through the word' (*dia-logos*) rather than 'in' words - to *point at* truths rather than to grasp or 'represent' them.

Hinting *hallows* the spoken word with silence, surrounding it with the aura or 'halo' of our listening awareness and giving it depth and wholeness. So also does proper *heeding,* as it gives time for a client's words and the questions they raise in us to sink in and penetrate us. The fact that we have heard a client out, that they have finished speaking for a while, by no means implies that we have heard their words out - that we have let someone's words speak to us and convey their own inner message. *Hearkening* is a silent listening contact and attunement to the *person,* one that begins even before the first word is spoken. *Heeding* is an inner receptivity and attunement to *language,* one that only comes to fruition after the last word has been spoken.

Listening is always more than just taking turns in speaking. It is the maturation of what is pregnant in silence. The extension of the interval between speaking challenges our capacity to be with others in silence, to simply 'be-a-body' rather than justifying or affirming ourselves in speech. It challenges us to temporarily suspend our speaking self, its personality and ego, and dwell instead in the 'listening self'. For it is only by restraining the social urge to respond to others immediately in speech - to agree or disagree, believe or disbelieve - that we give time for pre-conceptional intuitions and embryonic images to gather and incubate within us, and that we give ourselves time to *hold* and *behold* these impressions and images in our inner gaze. *Withholding* transforms *holding* into *beholding,* inward listening into inner seeing. It allows us to make genuine listening contact with the other by first *hearkening* to the silence that precedes speech. It is through *withholding* also that we give both ourselves and the speaker an opportunity to *heed* what has been said - to let the words which have been spoken linger in the air and speak to us after they have been spoken. It is in this way that listening allows us to behold the gathering (*legein*) of the 'inner word' (*logos*) and to 'read' or 'glean' its message (*lesen*).Herein lies the resonance of maieutic listening with the saying of Heraclitus, the first philosopher and psychologist of listening.

'Although this logos is timeless, men fail to comprehend it, both before hearing it and after they have heard'.

Introduction to Maieutic Analysis

To hear what is silent requires a hearing that each of us has
and no-one uses correctly.

Martin Heidegger

Maieutic analysis is the name I give to a new form of training
analysis and supervision for listening professionals. This includes not
only psychoanalysts, therapists or counsellors but all those whose
professional work has a strong listening component - for example
social workers, doctors and nurses, teachers and managers. Like
psychoanalysis, maieutic analysis is conducted one-to-one or in
small groups. Unlike personal analysis or therapy however, its focus
is not so much on the personal world of the analysand as on the
relationship between the latter and his or her professional clients.
The work of the maieutic analyst can be compared with that of the
individual to whom the professional practitioner goes for
professional supervision, but with two main differences:

(a) that this supervision does itself constitute a specific form of
training analysis, one principally focused on the analysand's way of
listening to others, and

(b) that because of its focus on styles of listening is not limited to
followers or trainees of a particular school of psychology,
psychoanalysis or therapy. Instead it is open to both lay persons from
a variety of professions and to already trained practitioners from a
wide variety of professional training backgrounds.

The maieutic analyst is a listening mentor, listening coach and
listening supervisor. He or she is also a listening analyst in the literal
sense: focused on the analysand's listening and analysing that
listening. Here the word 'analysis' is used in its original sense,
deriving from the Greek *analuein* - to 'loosen' or 'free up'. The
purpose of maieutic analysis is to deepen the analysand's listening
by (a) hearing the personal and professional parameters in which it
operates and (b) working to *loosen* these parameters where they
function in a restrictive or foreclosing way. This requires sensitivity
to the character of an individual's listening and its characterological
restrictions. This is an aspect of maieutic analysis influenced by the
work of Wilhelm Reich on character and character analysis. Reich

was the first psychoanalyst to take seriously the bodily dimension of psychoanalysis. He observed characteristic bodily postures and patterns of 'muscular armouring' in his clients, which he saw as their 'frozen history'. The maieutic analyst is, in a similar way, sensitive to the inner bearing or 'posture' of the listener - their frozen history and frozen training. A restrictive inner bearing finds its reflection not only in body language and physical posture but in 'linguistic armouring'. Linguistic armouring consists of automatic and stereotypical phrases with which a listener re-presents to themselves in language what comes to presence in their listening. These automatic phrases may be part of the practitioner's personal language and mental lexicon or they may belong to a terminology borrowed from others or internalised in the course of their professional training. The maieutic analyst is not neutral to the individual practitioner's characteristic listening style, inner bearing or language - particularly where the latter reveals a restrictive listening vocabulary, agenda or technique, or where it substitutes for an authentic capacity for 'being with'. Nor does the maieutic analyst respond from another ideological position. The basic 'position' or 'posture' of the maieutic analyst is not an intellectual, emotional or physical stance but a particular inner bearing - that of the midwife who listens with her whole being and whose listening sensitivity is rooted in the belly or *hara*. The maieutic analyst is above all someone capable of listening maieutically - of *hearkening and heeding, holding* and *withholding, harbouring* and *hinting*. It is through the depth and intensity of the analyst's own listening that a shift is gradually induced in the gravitational centre of the analysand's own listening.

Maieutic analysis depends on the analyst's capacity to fully *embody* his or her own listening self during the analytic session, thereby modelling and acting as a midwife for the analysand's own listening self. This means taking a stand and holding to a position beneath one's own speaking self - one's voice persona, language mind and linguistic ego or 'I'. The benefit of maieutic analysis is that the analysand gradually comes to sense the contrast between his or her own centre of gravity and inner bearing as a listener and the inner bearing of *maieusis*. The latter is achieved by the discipline of withholding. This is far more than a mere therapeutic technique or style based on 'minimal response' and 'acceptance of silence'. What is crucial is the quality of inner responsiveness, inner contact and communication achieved within that silence - the cultivation of a new experience of listening as an active 'inner voice communication'.

Evaluating the Therapist as Listener
- a Phenomenological Guide

The listener's capacity for 'withholding'

Does the listener jump in to fill gaps of silence whenever they occur, whether before, during or after you speak? Or are they capable of maintaining a receptive and attuned silence - again, not only while you are speaking or while you pause to reflect, but before you utter your first words ('hearkening' to silence) and after you have finished your 'turn' ('heeding' what has been said)? If they are able to keep silence, are they really there in that silence, with you? Or do their words and body language betray a disembodied mind or restless body? Are they capable of *being*-in-silence with you, just 'being-a-body' - or do they need to 'be somebody' - to affirm their professional role and impose their own listening agenda?

The listener's capacity for 'hearkening'

Does the listener sense where you 'are' even before you begin to speak - are they tuned into you in a way which encourages you to express what is really important to you at any given time? Do they sense your mood and state of being - whatever is pregnant in the silence that precedes any verbal exchange? Are they attuned to the qualities or 'tones' of silence or merely waiting in anticipation of your words? If you have difficulty in articulating what is going on in you, do they give sufficient time for you to find the right words, tone of voice and tone of language with which to speak authentically *from* yourself - communicating your inner tone and state of being? Or are they satisfied if you merely talk *about* yourself using whatever phrases you find ready to hand? They may *listen* to you. But do they listen to *you* - do you feel them making inner contact with you as they listen, hearing *you* and not just *hearing* you?

The listener's capacity for 'heeding'
Quite simply: does the listener take the *hint*? Do they give themselves time to respond inwardly to the implicit as well as explicit message conveyed by your words? Are they sensitive not only to your tone of voice and body language but to the tonality and 'voice' of your language itself? Can they hear if your language is not an authentic expression of your own being but borrowed, if its voice is not your voice but that of your parents or peers? Is the voice of their language truly their own or merely the voice of their particular professional 'in-group' and its language?

The listener's capacity for 'homing in'
Is the listener capable of picking up or 'homing in on' those words or references in your discourse which conceal more than they reveal - indicating areas which you would like to go into but need prompting and support to do so? Above all, can they hear in what you say not just what you say but that which you most fear to say - and fear to hear *said* to you? Can they bear and contain that which you still find un-bearable - can they *hold* this in their silence and *hint* at it in their verbal responses? Or are they unable to bear and say it themselves?

The listener's capacity for 'holding'
Can the listener continue to *hearken* while you are speaking, so that you not only feel that they are attending to what you say and how, but feel *held* in the inner gaze of their listening intent? Do you feel that it is you - your whole being - that they are in contact with? Is the listener capable not only of 'sympathetic' hearing and 'empathic' understanding, but of not-hearing and not-understanding - of hearing *you* rather than getting lost in what you say? Do they make a point of showing (through 'appropriate' words and body language) that they 'hear' and 'understand' you or do they genuinely 'under-stand' i.e. taking their stand *under* language and on the inner ground of their own being?

The listener's capacity for 'beholding'
Do you feel that the listener is looking inside themselves as they listen, or do they only look *at* or *for* you with their eyes - attempting to 'read' your body signals and feelings? Do you feel that the insights shared by the listener express a genuine 'in-sight' - a

capacity to hold and 'be-hold' pre-verbal impressions and images - or that they are verbal constructions which spring ready made from the listener's intellect and emotions, without any pre-verbal or pre-conceptual awareness?

The listener's capacity for 'taking to heart'

Taking to heart is a deeper form of *heeding* - the listener's willingness to undergo an emotional transformation, to be touched by your words. Such 'empathy' is not automatic. It takes time to *heed* and acknowledge the *pathos* of someone's words as the expression of questions or dilemmas, desires or emotions, strengths or weaknesses that they share with you. *Taking to heart* involves even more than this however, for it requires a willingness on the part of the listener to hear in you an echo of selves they do not know - aspects of 'them-selves' that they are not fully familiar with. A listener who *takes to heart* is able not only to find a meaning for themselves in what you say but to find something of value to them in the way that you say it - to appreciate and value the part of them that you embody and speak for. Key questions therefore: does the listener acknowledge 'we-meanings' in what you say or treat all issues as your private property or private problems? Do they acknowledge you as speaking *for* them as well as to them? Can they find value as well as meaning in what you say, appreciating the qualities you embody for them as well as the meanings you express to them?

The listener's capacity for 'harbouring'

Do you feel that the listener's questions communicate their inner listening responsiveness or do they merely compensate for a lack of intuitive responsiveness? Do they hit the mark? If so, they will ask questions which *say* something rather than merely asking for something to be said, questions which not only ask for a response but are a response. Questions that are full rather than empty shells. Questions that the listener does not hide behind but communicates through. A listener capable of 'harbouring' a question is one who does not even need to verbalise it to evoke a response from us. Instead we sense the questing intent harboured and communicated by their listening. Only such a listener is able also to *formulate* suggestive and penetrating questions. For a listener who 'harbours' gives time for questions to first gather and gestate, to formulate themselves. Are the listener's questions precisely and insightfully formulated? Or are they merely formulaic? Does the listener give you time to come to an inner awareness of implicit questions in your own time, through silent inward listening and through hearing yourself speak - or do their questions force you into a premature explicitness?

The listener's capacity for 'holding open'
Are the listener's 'open questions' really open, or are they part of some hidden diagnostic or interpretative listening agenda - a way of answering the listener's own closed questions? Do you feel that the listener really *heeds* your own questions, stated or implied, as open questions, or does their own listening agenda foreclose these questions? Does their listening raise into view new questions or restrict itself to the scope of questions already raised? Do you feel that the listener somehow helps you to enter the realm of feeling and experience opened up by questions - to get closer to yourself on a wordless level - or do their questions draw you *out* of your depths and into the realm of superficial and stereotyped language? Do you feel a patient reverence in the listener for your own profound depths and the open mysteries of being? Or do you feel the listener containing this mystery in the closed book of their own familiar phraseology, associations and symbolism?

The listener's capacity for 'hosting'
Do you feel that the listener is exclusively focused on you, or that the listener is also very much in touch with themselves and with the 'Between'? Do you feel that the listener is only listening to you, or that, being with this listener, it is as if you are both listening to this Between, both opening yourselves to a source of insight that is neither purely personal, nor even preoccupied with the inter-personal, but has its source in a 'trans-personal' or 'spiritual' dimension? If so, this is testament to the listener's capacity for 'hosting'.

The listener's 'hara'
The listener's willingness to 'under-go' a transformation depends on their willingness to 'go under' - to first find a ground within themselves that is deeper and firmer than either thoughts or feelings.

Does the listener respond from their head or their heart, their reason or emotions, with both, or from some place deeper? A listener whose centre of gravity is neither the head nor the heart but the belly or 'hara' is one whose embodied presence expresses meditative inner silence and stillness, whose listening communicates *groundedness* and *gravitas*. This enables them to listen intensively, intuitively and with a wordless inner knowing that is not confused with concepts or named emotions, nor with sophisticated psycho-babble. A listener with *hara* works on us silently with their whole being - slowing our rate of speech, making us more patient in listening to ourselves before we speak, helping us to hear our own words in a deeper way after they are spoken. Their *being* there with us has a quality that helps us listen to our own being. This recalls the words of Meister Eckhart:

'Nothing will work of whatever works
they work who are not great in being.'

Listening and Cultural Mythology

The myth of our culture: that it is by opening our mouths and speaking, expressing ourselves or asking each other questions, making small talk or telling stories - in a word, through speech and language - that we establish contact with another human being and open the channels of communication. What if the opposite is true - namely that it is in silence that we establish real inner contact with another human being - a silence in which we lean or list our whole being towards the being of the other, in which we *list-en*?

The myth of our culture: that listening can be reduced to a set of communicative or counselling 'skills'. As if it made no difference *who* was listening to us, so long as they listened in the 'right' way, adopting the 'right' body language and making the 'right' noises. What if the opposite is true: namely that 'We hear not the ear', that listening cannot be separated from *being*, and that in listening with our whole being, we also communicate our whole being - who we are?

The myth of our culture: that we listen *because* someone is speaking to us and in order to respond 'after-words'. As if the speaker would even begin to speak to us were it not first clear to them that in some way we were already listening - even before a word was uttered. What then, if the opposite is true, namely that what is said to us is itself a response - an 'effect' of the way we are listening?

The myth of our culture: that listening is something we do only *while* someone is speaking. As if the listening contact we establish with another human being even *before* they begin to speak played no part in shaping a dialogue and setting its tone. As if we could truly *hear* what another is saying without first hearkening to the silence preceding their words. As if the time we grant ourselves to fully heed and take in another person's words *after* they have spoken were not equally a part of what we call 'listening'.

The myth of our culture: that conversation is a function of speech and consists in people taking turns in speaking. As if any meaningful exchange could take place without people listening to themselves and others. What if the opposite is true: that dialogue depends principally on our capacity for being-in-silence with others, and for tolerating an interval of silence *between* speaking turns?

The myth of our culture: that it is language and speech that *let's things be said*. As if there were anything we could say or that could be said to us without our listening being open to it. What if it is not speaking but listening that first lets things be said to us? What if language merely *re*-presents what listening itself allows to come to presence?

The myth of our culture: that we 'think' in language. What if the opposite is true? What if thinking is rooted not in speech and language but in the listener's silent attunement and wordless understanding? What if language is itself the translation of this wordless understanding? What if what we call 'thinking' is the very process of translating what our inner listening attunement brings silently to light?

Keywords in Maieutic Listening

Withholding - the capacity to restrain immediate verbal response and extend the interval of silence between speaking 'turns'.

Hearkening - focusing on the still-point of silence within ourselves and establishing an 'umbilical' telepathic connection from the **hara**.

Homing in - the capacity to establish a precise listening tone and 'wavelength' of attunement as one listens, from which impressions and images can surface.

Harbouring - the capacity to **withhold** from verbal questioning of the speaker and instead to **hold** and **heed** our own questions silently within ourselves.

Holding Open - the capacity to hold questions open within ourselves, and allow answers time to incubate, rather than needing to come to conclusions.

Hallowing - **withholding** after someone has finished speaking, thus letting their words linger 'in the air' and sink into us in silence. Only in this way can we **heed** a person's choice of words and language as well as attuning to their inner being.

Heeding - letting the speaker's words sink in and penetrate us so that we take them to heart. This can take moments, hours or years. It implies that we are able to hear another person's words as the echo of a part of oneself, irrespective of whether we agree or disagree with them.

Hypnosis - the Greek word for sleep. Listening understood as a 'hypnotic' state in which we allow ourselves to 'sleep into' the speech of the other.

Hara - listening from the belly rather than from the head or heart. This means breathing abdominally, with the diaphragm rather than the chest muscles.

Holding - just as one can hold someone in one's visual gaze, so one can hold them in the inner gaze of one's listening intent.

Handling - silently messaging the speaker by modulating the inner 'tone' of one's listening and the inner 'touch' of one's listening intent.

Beholding - the capacity to turn one's gaze inward as one listens and 'hold' the inner impressions that gather and come into view.

Hosting - the altered quality of self-experience that comes about through suspending the ordinary speaking self and becoming host to one's own inner 'listening self'.

THE THERAPIST AS LISTENER

A Missing Dimension of Counselling
and Psychotherapy Training

Despite the central importance that listening obviously holds in the therapeutic relationship, the training of counsellors, therapists and health professionals rarely focuses on the nature of the practitioner's own *listening praxis and process*, concentrating instead on the application of specific sets of paradigmatic skills, terminologies, techniques, models and 'methodologies' in the therapeutic relationship. As a result, trainee or newly-trained practitioners tend to hear only what they are *trained* to hear within the framework of these theoretical models and methodologies, and listening itself is reduced to a set of practical skills or techniques subordinated to them. Their will to *help* others may find expression in the application of skills and techniques but often does so at the expense of the will and capacity to truly hear. If healing begins with being heard, then it is essential that the *will to hear* not be subordinated to the *will to help* and its instruments.

Within the psychotherapeutic literature there has been no attempt to formulate a *language of listening* independent of the terminologies employed within different schools of psychotherapy and counselling. Aside from the work of Reik and Langs it is also hard to find any significant appreciation of listening itself as an *active* form of inner communication between practitioner and client. Nor have specific means of counselling and therapy training been developed which focus on the therapist or counsellor as *listener* rather than as practitioner of a specific form of 'talking cure'. This paradoxical and highly questionable situation is aggravated by the fact that there are, on the other hand, a number of core assumptions about the very nature of listening and its role in human communication which pervade the language of therapy and counselling. These core assumptions can, I believe, actively hinder the training of counsellors and therapists, and the cultivation of what I call *deep hearing*. Practitioners, whether therapists or counsellors, who emerge from their training without an awareness of their own personal *listening process and praxis*, may end up using their own institutionally framed skills and knowledge as a highly effective defence against deep hearing - often at high cost to their clients.

What I call 'maieutic analysis' is a new form of training and supervision for therapists and counsellors focusing specifically on their own personal listening process and praxis and designed to complement their existing professional training and experience. It also provides trainers and training institutions with a simple but powerful medium for developing a new understanding and experience of the therapist as listener - one that can overcome an important gap in the repertoire and resources of existing training programmes. The focus of 'maieutic analysis' is the cultivation of what I call 'maieutic listening' (from the Greek *maieuesthai* - to 'act as a midwife'). The language of maieutic listening is the result of over 20 years of phenomenological research into the philosophy and psychology of listening. The phenomenological basis of this research was not merely the listening experiences of therapists and counsellors but the experience of those they listen to - the client's own experience of the therapist as listener.

Maieutic listening requires not only an understanding but an active embodiment of insights from many sources, including Heidegger, Winnicott, Reik and Reich. Before I introduce the philosophical underpinning and praxis of maieutic listening in more depth, however, it is important to look at its flip-side: the core assumptions currently governing our understanding of therapeutic listening and the consequences these assumptions have for the client when they are unreflectively accepted and applied. The core assumptions I refer to are nothing extraordinary - they are simply the reflection in counselling and psychotherapy of many accepted everyday beliefs about listening - beliefs of a sort we find embedded in everyday language and quite generally embodied in everyday modes of relating.

Fundamental beliefs about listening and their reflection in counselling and therapy

1. *Listening is something we 'do'.* This is the basic belief that allows listening to be reduced to some sort of technique-bound communication 'skill'. Grounded listening is based on an understanding of listening not as an ordinary form of 'doing' but as a capacity to *be* with and 'bear with' ourselves and others in pregnant silence, to make inner contact with our own being and other beings. Without a mature capacity on the part of the practitioners to *be* with themselves and others in silence and to bear whatever thoughts and feelings are pregnant in that silence - not needing to express *or* repress them - the client's own difficulties in bearing with and bearing forth those thoughts and feelings will be enhanced.

2. *We listen to others.* The implicit assumption here is that we can listen to others without at the same time listening to ourselves, be in touch with others without staying in touch with ourselves, be fully present to others without being fully present to ourselves. But by thinking that the entire focus of their listening attention must be on the client, practitioners find themselves forced to parcel off a portion of what they are feeling or thinking and hold this in reserve for supervision sessions. Clients will automatically sense if their therapist or counsellor is not fully in touch with themselves as they listen - unable to process their own inner responses, or feeling torn between expressing them verbally or parcelling them off as material for supervision.

3. *We listen in order to be able to respond.* The core assumption dominating most forms of therapeutic listening and counselling practice, as well as medical practice and psychiatry, is that listening is merely a *necessary prelude* to some form of outward, verbal response to the client - whether in the form of empathic insights and 'mirroring', analytic interpretation, or medical-psychiatric diagnosis. Operating on this assumption, however, practitioners will inevitably be perceived as only 'half there' as listeners, the other half being preoccupied with the attempt to fulfil a professional role and formulate an adequate professional response. This assumption ignores the fact that (a) what a client says to us and the way they say

it is *already* a response to the way we are listening - or not listening - to them and (b) conversely, the way we hear what someone is saying to us itself *says* something to them. In other words, our way of inwardly perceiving another person is always picked up and perceived by that person, whether consciously or not, just as our *inner listening response* to another person is borne back to that person in silence - whether or not we express it outwardly.

It requires considerable courage on the part of the practitioners to recognise this fact i.e. to be fully aware of the silent communication that is mediated by the listening process and to actively *relate* to the client through it - consciously 'bearing back' (*re-latere*) what they hear and perceive in silence. But whereas clients invariably 'pick up' the listener's innermost response to them, expressed or unexpressed, many practitioners lack *faith* in the reality of this inner communication - needing to 'prove' to the client that they have really heard them. Alternatively, they may feel *safe* with their clients only by believing that their innermost responses, if they are not expressed, remain unperceived. Either way, this lack of *confidence* in the silent communication of listener and client puts implicit pressure on the latter to *conceal or ignore* their own inner perceptions of this communication - the silent messages they are getting from the practitioner - complying instead with the communicational framework or 'language games' imposed on the therapeutic relationship *by* the practitioner.

4. *We listen to persons.* Listening to the person, even the 'whole person', is not the same as listening to the inner human *being*, let alone the whole human being. The client as a person is the particular face of the individual that presents itself to the practitioner - one face amongst others. No therapist or counsellor would agree to conducting a session with a client by *proxy* - for example by seeing a parent or partner, friend or colleague of the latter instead. And yet how many practitioners, particularly those with a 'person-centred' orientation, are aware that the person in front of them may be a *proxy persona* and that when the client talks *about* him- or herself, albeit in the first person, this is effectively a type of report on a *third person*, one whose voice is never directly heard and whose face or faces remain invisible to the listener. The word 'client' means 'one who calls'. If someone has an accident in the street, breaks their leg and

cries for help, it is easy to hear and see who is calling. But what if the call is silent or coded, and the one who calls invisible or mute? It requires a different type of listening to hear *this* call, to respond to the true 'client' rather than a proxy persona, and to avoid the temptation of entering into a relatively comfortable 'third person' conversation *about* the client rather than relating directly to them. Here again, clients themselves are often less bound by the core assumption than their professional listeners. They are often *aware* if the practitioner mistakes their social masks or *personae* for their inner self. One reason why they may be in therapy or counselling in the first place is precisely because this is their general experience of relationships - of remaining unseen and unheard, however much and however consciously they try and signal their own hidden feeling, betray the cracks in the mask and hint at the presence of voices within them that are as yet unexpressed and unheard. There is a world of difference between engaging in a therapeutic conversation with a client and hearing an *unspoken dialogue* that occurs within the client and between the different inner voices of client and practitioner.

5. *We listen to people's words.* One of the major paradoxes of verbal communication in general, and of therapeutic communication in particular, is that we can never fully represent *in* words what it is that we are saying to others *through* them (*dia-logos*). This dia-logical dimension of meaning has to do not only with what the speaker means to say through their words but what they mean to the listener. In a psychoanalytic context the attempt to interpret the covert messages or 'sub-texts' of spoken communication, whilst perfectly valid as a therapeutic instrument, does not escape the basic paradox. For every verbal response to a sub-text on the part of the practitioner will itself carry its *own* sub-text - saying more *through* the word than it represents in words. Psychoanalysis is the paradigm of a type of listening designed to attune the listener to sub-texts and dia-logical communication. But the first requirement for this type of listening is not interpretative skills but rather the capacity to *withhold* verbal responses of any sort - allowing an interval in which what has been *said* through the word is fully received, wordlessly and in silence. The unspoken is not what is 'unsaid' - it is precisely what is said rather than spoken, communicated *through* the word rather than

in it. 'Not knowing how to listen, neither can they speak.' (Heraclitus). Practitioners who miss this distinction often confuse the unsaid with the unspoken. The result is that they try to immediately represent the client's unspoken sub-texts *in* words without first giving themselves time to take in and fully heed what the client has actually *said* to them through these words - acknowledging a message which holds meaning for them as well as for the client. The client's main aim is not to have what they are *saying* clarified or conceptualised, represented or reformulated in the practitioner's own words (for through this their own sub-text will invariably be overlaid with a sub-text of the responding practitioner) but to *be heard* - to touch the listener through their words. Clients sense very easily if, when they have finished speaking, the practitioner has difficulty withholding immediate verbal responses and allowing a period of silence in which to absorb what has been said in silence. Yet unless the practitioner is capable of this sort of restraint, the client is deprived of a vital opportunity to hear what they themselves have said - to let their *own* words echo within and reveal new dimensions of meaning. We do not help others to hear themselves more deeply by responding to what they have said but by fully hearing it and taking it to heart, heeding it and holding on to it in silence. Only through such patient *withholding* do we first come to actually *behold* what has been said - to feel and see what we ourselves have heard.

6. *We listen to others while they are speaking.* 'Although this *logos* holds forever, men fail to comprehend it, both before hearing it and once they have heard.' (Heraclitus). As I have already emphasised, what is said to us by others is already a response to the way we are listening to others - to the listening attunement we establish not just while we hear them speak but *before* and *after* they speak. The parent does not listen simply because the child is speaking. The child speaks, and speaks in a certain way, because he senses that the parent is listening, and listening in a certain way. If the child senses the parent is not tuned in before he or she begins to speak, its language and tone of voice will be different. If the parent responds in an unattuned way after the child has spoken, the latter will feel restrained in saying more. Our listening attunement to others, no less than our spoken words, carries its own intonation, reflecting the wavelength of attunement to the speaker. The silent tone of the

practitioner's listening is echoed in their tone of voice when they respond to the client. But it is also sensed in silence by the client, both before and after the latter speaks. *Without* inner awareness of the *tone* of their listening, the practitioner cannot alter this tone and use it as a carrier wave of silent communication with the client. *With* awareness of their own listening intonation, practitioner's can modulate the tone of their listening, convey subtle messages through it, and use it to help *tune the client in* to new tones of feeling and different voices within themselves.

7. *Listening means attending to others when they speak.* The fact that I *hear* you does not guarantee that I hear *you* - the being that speaks. Nor does it guarantee that *I* hear you - that I let your words speak to me and touch my being. Counsellors and therapists are trained to *attend* to many 'things' - to many levels and dimensions of communication. But it is precisely 'some-thing' we *attend* to. The truth is that whilst we can attend to some-thing we cannot attend to some-one, to a being. But we can *intend* that being - really mean them. There is a basic difference between using speech to mean or say 'something' and using it to address someone - to convey a message to a specific other. I can ask someone what they are trying to say to *me* - what message they are trying to give me and whether it is really *me* they mean with this message. What is true of speech is true also of listening. The client will sense if the practitioner's listening intent is really tuned to them as a being - really 'means' them - or whether it is a type of listening attention that could equally well be applied to someone else and is essentially focused on some 'thing' or other. We all know if someone is listening to and hearing *us* or not or whether they are merely attending to us and listening 'in role'. In professional contexts it is all the more important to understand that it is not simply our attentiveness as listeners that counts but its intentionality, and specifically, our capacity to *intend* this other. Only through intending *this* human being and not any other can listening become a medium of intimate inner contact and communication between human beings.

We live in a culture that knows only two types of intimacy - that achieved through talk and verbal communication and that achieved through touch and physical contact. In the context of psychotherapy and counselling training it is above all important for practitioners to acknowledge the type of intimate contact and communication that can be established through listening itself, rather than through talk or touch. For by establishing inner listening contact and communication with their clients they help the latter to experience this type of spiritual intimacy with others themselves. If on the other hand, the practitioner is incapable of establishing this inner listening contact and communication with their clients, no amount of talking can replace it, nor will either practitioner or client be inwardly touched by one another through this talk. The practitioner will be dependent on words or body language to establish and maintain 'rapport', whilst the client will be inwardly conscious of the superficiality or artificiality of the emotional 'closeness' thus achieved.

8. *Listening and looking go hand in hand.* It has become a modern cliché that eighty-percent of human communication is 'non-verbal', and that listening therefore goes together with looking at others as they speak and attending to their 'body language'. There is an implicit identification of non-verbal communication with visual cues and clues. The crude dichotomy of 'verbal' and 'non-verbal' communication ignores the fact that verbal communication can itself be understood as non-verbal in its very essence, for this essence has to do with the wordless messages and soundless voices that communicate through a person's speech. To truly *see* what I am hearing my listening gaze must be focused inwardly not outwardly. One of the hardest and most controversial parts of my work with therapists and counsellors is to persuade them that sitting opposite, staring at or seeking eye-contact with a client whilst they are speaking is *not* at all conducive to taking in what the client is *saying*. Nor does it allow the practitioner an opportunity to listen and look into *themselves* as they listen to a client - the only way in which genuine *in-sight* is born.

Many clients do not make eye-contact with their therapist or counsellor as they speak, or meet their gaze only intermittently. That is not because they are schizoid but because their gaze is turned inward - they are *listening* to themselves. But when practitioners insist on holding their client in their visual gaze this is often because they have not experienced what it means to hold someone in the *inner gaze of their listening*. The client may feel encouraged or inhibited by the practitioner's visual gaze. At the same time, however, unless they meet this gaze and make eye-contact with the listener they are also reduced to an object by it. Nobody wants to be looked at whilst sitting on a psychological toilet seat. No listener needs to stare at or make eye-contact with a client whilst the latter is engaged in processing and expressing powerful feelings and emotions. This can only be a distraction for the client, and is often used by counsellors and therapists only to seek a narcissistic reflection and confirmation of their own being. Eye-contact with a client as a they speak does not say 'I see you'. It says 'please see *me*' - affirm that I am here too and affirm me in my role. At the very least it says 'I cannot feel myself in contact with you by just *listening* to you.' This message is itself the expression of a number of different beliefs about listening I have already examined. One is the belief that we can listen to others without listening to ourselves - for listening to ourselves means *looking inside* ourselves as we listen, just as the client does. Another is the belief that listening is purely a mode of attention. The listener who wholeheartedly *attends* to me as I speak - all ears and all eyes - may be genuinely interested, sympathetic and empathic. Such a listener may make me *feel* as if I am being heard. But feeling heard is not the same thing as being heard. And nor is making people *feel* that they are being heard (a principal focus of 'listening skills' training) the same thing as actually *hearing* them.

In ordinary conversation, looking at others is a way of maintaining outer contact and communication, simultaneously affirming the other and seeking affirmation from them. But a therapist or counsellor needs to be someone of sufficient *maturity* to fully affirm their own being and that of the client without any need of narcissistic affirmation from the client - someone capable of continuously and consistently listening into themselves at the same time as they listen to others.

9. *Listening is a mental activity.* The idea that listening is a mental or 'cognitive' activity has particular significance in counselling and psychotherapy. It expresses itself in the practitioner's desire to mentally and emotionally 'connect' with what their clients are telling them and to 'make connections' between different elements of the client's story. But whilst it is recognised that the empathic and emotional dimension of listening has a bodily and physiological dimension, very little attention is usually paid to *the embodied*

presence of the practitioner - their capacity to fully be there as a body, to be 'some-body' and not just as a disembodied mind or consciousness.

Embodied listening is a capacity for attunement to our body's own wordless, felt senses of meaning. It involves not only being able to feel our own inner responses in a wordless, bodily way, but also being able to *bear with* and *body* those responses - to find an inner posture or 'bearing' that allows us to contain and process them.

The word 'session' means a 'sitting'. In a therapy session, practitioner and client sit together. The session is a sitting together. The practitioner's mental attitude to the client in the session is one thing. Their inner bearing is another, embodied in their very way of sitting with the client. To seat oneself in order to sit with a client in a session means far more than just sitting our bodies down on chairs. For a therapist to 'bear with' the client as listener - to bear the full weight or *gravitas* of the often 'grave' or 'heavy' questions they are confronted with - is impossible unless, in seating themselves, they do not lean their body forward towards the client but instead let their own body weight come fully to rest under gravity. Only in this way can they also *centre* both their awareness and their breathing in their abdomen - their own physical and spiritual centre of gravity. Deep listening is centred listening. It is also grounded listening. True seatedness is a way of sitting in which the therapist feels seated in the deep *inner ground* of their being, the only secure ground from which they can offer true 'support' to the client, comfortably bearing in a bodily way the full weight of the issues pressing down on or 'depressing' the latter.

Evaluating the therapist as listener - key criteria

The critical deconstruction of those generalised core assumptions about listening that still influence psychotherapy and counselling training has a positive and constructive side. It allows us to develop a new frame of reference for evaluating counsellors and therapists as listeners, one which is independent of particular approaches to therapy and counselling. What follows is a brief and highly condensed summary of the basic criteria which I believe are of central importance in evaluating a practitioner's way of listening to a client - something not to be confused with their skill in responding to a client in accordance with a specific training model.

The listener's capacity for 'being with themselves':
'Nothing will work of whatever works they work, who are not great in being.' (Meister Eckhart). Do you feel that the listener is fully *there* as a whole human being or rather that they are merely acting out a professional role, using their professional skills and personal empathy to listen 'in role'?

The listener's capacity for 'being with others':
Do you feel that the listener is fully with you as a human being, tuned not just to your outer personality but to the silent core of your being? Are they able to hear *through* your words as well as responding *to* them *in* words? Do you feel that they hear *you* and not just your words or expressed emotions; that they can *hearken* to the silence from which they emerge and *heed* the messages you wish to convey through them?

The listener's capacity for 'being alone with others':
Do you feel that the listener is able to be fully 'alone' or 'at-one' with themselves as they listen to you, or rather that their very attention to you is a way of distancing themselves from their own feelings, their own body and their own being? Is the listener able to remain fully at-one and at-ease with themselves independently of your own response to them, or do they directly or indirectly seek affirmation from you? (For example, by needing to impose a particular way of working on you, taking rejection of this way of

working as a rejection of them, or feeling ill-at-ease if it is *not* working.)

The listener's capacity for 'being-in-silence':
Does the listener jump in to fill intervals of silence, whether these occur before, during or after you speak? Do they become physically restless, tense and mentally abstracted and absented? Or are they capable of really staying with themselves and with you in silence - maintaining an embodied presence, sensitive to what may be pregnant in the silence, and capable of the type of *forbearance* that allows this silence to bear fruit in its own time?

The listener's capacity for 'being-a-body':
Is the listener capable of fully coming to rest in their own body and chair as they listen to you? Do you sense the listener's embodied presence as a being, feeling inwardly touched and held by it, or do you feel yourself turned into the mental or emotional object of a partly disembodied professional mind?

The listener's capacity for 'bearing with others':
Do you feel that the listener allows themselves to be inwardly touched by what you say and has the capacity to contain and 'bear' whatever feelings and inner responses it may evoke in them? Or do they rather give the impression of wanting to remain detached, placing a firm inner boundary between their feelings and yours, and turning both into neutralised objects? 'Bear with me' is another way of saying - 'please listen patiently to what I have to say'. But the client who comes to a counsellor or therapist may also be saying something else - 'there are facts or feelings that I find *unbearable*. Please relieve me of some of my burden by bearing or 'carrying' it with me'. Bearing with a client means more than just listening patiently. It requires a mature capacity to bear painful facts and feelings that the client themself finds unbearable. This is not the same as identifying with a client's *suffering*, letting oneself be overwhelmed by it or feeling that one has to share it. That is because bearing is essentially different from suffering. We *suffer* the unbearable not because we are forced to 'bear' it but precisely because we have not found a way to bear it, or cannot at this point bear it alone.

Listening is being and bearing with others in pregnant silence. Without a mature capacity to share in psychically containing and carrying another person's burden, to really feel its weight and *bear* that weight *with* them, the listener leaves them to suffer this burden alone. Worse still, if the listener is a counsellor or therapist to whom a person has come for help, they also give the latter the disheartening and demoralising message that even professional helpers regard their pain or suffering as essentially *unbearable*. The capacity to *bear with* automatically helps the latter to find a new *inner bearing* - one which allows them to bear their own burden in a new way, confronting otherwise unbearable facts and feelings which are a cause of suffering and pain. *Bearing with* requires a type of maturity that comes from the practitioner's own breadth and depth of feeling and life experience - something that no training programme can substitute for. I believe, however, that with the right sort of training, practitioners can find a new inner bearing themselves, one that gives their listening posture sufficient weight and *gravitas* to bear with their clients - to help them bear the unbearable.

The listener's capacity for 'bearing the question':
Do you feel that the listener is able to hearken to the implicit or explicit questions raised by what you tell them, to hold the *charge* of these questions in silence and in this way help you to do the same? Or do they immediately try to *hold off* and *foreclose* any questions evoked in them by putting these questions to you - hoping that the answers they elicit from you will promptly release the charge of the questions thus making it unnecessary for both of you to bear their full weight? At the heart of all the questions that clients bring to their therapists or counsellors are not just personal psychological issues but shared philosophical or 'trans-personal' questions - to do with the nature of life and death, health and sickness, responsibility and relationships. The listener's capacity to 'bear with others' depends also on their willingness to acknowledge the shared human questions expressed in the client's 'issues' - not treating them as the client's personal and private 'problem' but instead acknowledging their echo in the practitioner's own life and relationships. 'Bearing a question' means being prepared to experience that question as our own question as well as one belonging to the client. It means holding it

open within ourselves rather than passing the buck. The habit of immediately 'throwing back' questions raised in us by a client's presentation is a defence against bearing the question - experiencing it as a question for us too. The result of this defensive questioning on the part of the practitioner reinforces the client's feeling of isolation - the belief that the questions they confront are theirs alone, and that having them means there is something 'wrong' with them. If asked, no practitioner would concur with this belief theoretically. But the use of defensive questioning on the part of practitioners is by no means rare, and constitutes a habit that may actually be reinforced by their own professional training. Questions that practitioners are able to bear in silence within them and forbear from putting to the client in words will invariably communicate to the latter in silence, bringing their own answer in a short space of time. *Bearing the question* is therefore part and parcel of the practitioner's capacity to be and bear with others in silence.

Maieutic Listening and Maieutic Analysis

I began this article by stressing how curious it was that despite the centrality of listening to the therapeutic relationship, the nature of the practitioner's listening process and praxis is a subject that barely figures in the literature on therapy and counselling, and forms no major part of any training programme that I know of. Whilst language has become a central theme in psychoanalysis, the same cannot be said of listening. Nor has there been much attempt to develop an in-depth philosophy and psychology of listening. For this we require a phenomenological *language of listening*, one which acknowledges listening as a language in its own right, and one which is itself a *listening language* - rooted in a deepened experience of listening. To *think* the nature of therapeutic listening in a deeper way requires a thinking which is itself an expression of deep listening. The language of listening I have presented here - the language of 'being' and 'bearing' - was inspired by the work of Martin Heidegger, a thinker, who, like Heraclitus, understood thinking itself as a listening process and praxis.

Maieutic listening is a therapeutic listening *praxis* rooted in a language of listening whose central metaphor is the listener as *midwife*. The praxis of maieutic listening is not merely the expression of a new theoretical posture however. It requires the active *embodiment* of a new inner bearing - that of the restrained and forbearing midwife. When a woman is pregnant, her physical centre of gravity lowers, and she needs to find a physical posture and bearing able to accommodate this lowered centre and bear her own increased weight. Something similar is true of people who come to therapy psychologically 'pregnant' - carrying a heavy psychological burden which oppresses them because they can neither psychically bear it nor abort and terminate it.

The relation between the client's ego and outer persona on the one hand, and their innermost being or 'self' on the other, can be compared to the relation between a pregnant mother and the as-yet unborn being she bears within her womb. The role of the midwife is not just to 'attend' to the mother and her needs, but also to the needs of the child she carries. Similarly, the role of the listener *as* midwife is not just to attend to the person of the client but to make contact with the being they carry or bear within them - the inner human being. To do so the listener must be in continuous listening contact *with* their own inner being, and learn to listen inwardly *from* their inner being. Training in maieutic listening focuses on cultivating an experience of listening as a medium of 'core' contact and communication with others. Maieutic listening is contactful and communicative listening, an embodiment of what I call 'core-relatedness' rather than ego-relatedness. It is also *grounded* listening, rooted not in the person of the listener, their head or heart, but in the silent core of their being - their spiritual centre of gravity or *hara*. As such it stands in marked contrast to a type of listening dominated by the core assumptions I listed above.

- It is based on a resolute subordination of the *will-to-help* to the *will-to-hear*, rather than vice versa. Its aim is not so much to hear others in order to help them but to help them to hear themselves.

- Its focus is not so much on the person speaking as on the person's own relationship to their inner being - their way of listening to themselves before and after they speak, their capacity to make contact with their inner being and respond to its inner voice.

- It is not so much a mode of listening *attention* to another person as the embodiment of the listener's active *intent* to make inner listening contact with the silent core of another human being.

- It recognises that different wavelengths of attunement to others each bear their own silent *tone*; that the tone of our listening automatically communicates to others, and that therefore listening can become an active form of silent communication - bearing messages which ride on the tone of our listening and which bear back our inner perceptions of others.

Educating the therapist as listener - training in maieutic listening

Training in maieutic listening is oriented around the criteria for evaluating 'the therapist as listener' outlined above. For each of these I have developed extremely pair exercises designed to both challenge and strengthen the practitioner's capacity to 'listen' in the most essential sense - to *be-a-body,* to,*be-in-silence*, and to thereby truly *bear-with-others* in that silence. In describing evaluation criteria for the 'therapist as listener' I posed them as questions in the second person - 'Did you feel that your listener was able to...?' This is in order to show how such questions can also be put to use in professional training contexts - for example as questions put to trainee counsellors and therapists after taking on the 'role' of client in pair-practice with their peers, or in taking on the role of observer in training 'triads'. The questions can also function as guidelines for the creation of 'reverse case studies' - not case notes written by a trainee counsellor or therapist in their role *as* counsellor or therapist but rather written from their own experience of *being a client* and *being listened to* by another - whether an actual or trainee therapist or counsellor. This 'reverse case study' method can be complemented by what I call 'reverse supervision'. Here the trainer or supervisor themselves chooses a number of personal issues that he or she is prepared to share with the trainee, talks about them openly and in this way gains a *direct* personal experience of the trainee's own bearing and comportment as a listener.

'Maieutic analysis' is the term I have used to name a new type of complementary training and supervision in therapeutic listening - understood as *maieusis*. Another term I have used for training and supervision in maieutic listening is 'third ear education'. The concept of an 'inner' or 'third ear' is nothing exotic or esoteric. For as Heidegger emphasised '*We* hear, not the ear.' The 'third ear' is the ear with which *we* listen and not just our ears. It is the ear with which we listen with and from our whole body and whole being - rather than our head or heart alone. It is the ear with which we hearken to the inner human being rather than merely hearing the outer 'person'. It is the inner ear through which we become 'all ear'. As 'third ear education', maieutic listening is a way to fully *embody* Heidegger's understanding that a truly 'grounded listening' is 'an abiding with the inner ear.'

THERAPY AND PHILOSOPHY

A DIALOGUE

S: scholar R: researcher T: therapist

S: Why do you believe Heidegger's thinking is so important for psychotherapy, for the training of psychotherapists, indeed for the health of society?

R: Above all, because his is a philosophy of listening and a listening philosophy - one in which thinking itself is defined as a type of listening, and in which listening in turn is understood as a fundamental dimension of our being. Our current global culture on the other hand, is one in which the speaking self is valued more than the listening self, in which linguistic and mathematical skills are valued more than listening skills, and in which truth is ever more narrowly identified with its scientific representation in words, numbers and images.

T: Heidegger's philosophy is often described as a 'fundamental ontology', from the Greek *ontos* - 'being'. You imply that Heidegger's understanding of listening was an ontological rather than a conventional psychological or physiological one.

R: That is true. Listening, for Heidegger, is essentially linked to what in German is called Dasein and Mitsein - 'being there'' and 'being with'. To listen is above all to really be there for another human being and not to withdraw behind a role or set of listening 'techniques'. It is also to really be with that person - to make contact with their essential being.

T: I fear that a lot of people, including a lot of psychotherapists, would have difficulty grasping exactly what this means.

R: If by 'grasping' we mean being able to represent it in other words or in mental images you are no doubt right. But that brings us to Heidegger's essential point, namely that thinking itself is something more than a mere capacity to grasp and represent meanings in words or images.

S: If thinking is not the mental representation of reality, what is it?

R: To quote Heidegger: 'Thinking is a listening that brings something into view ... something one can hear. In doing so it brings into view what was unheard-of.' This 'bringing' into view does not mean representing something in words or images. Indeed it can only come about if, on the contrary, we suspend all the words and images that pass through our mind as we listen to someone.

T: I think we can all understand the point that as soon as someone begins to speak we begin to seek to represent to ourselves in some way what they are saying.

R: Indeed even before someone begins to speak, our listening might already be shaped by a framework of possible representations that shape and circumscribe our hearing.

S: But surely it is impossible to enter into a dialogue without any anticipatory representation of what might be said. The context of the dialogue itself will imply certain general themes and purposes, will take place within a particular universe of discourse and be shaped by a common language.

R: For Heidegger, listening meant above all what could be called a non-representational anticipation of what there is to be said.

S: I am not quite sure what 'non-representational anticipation' could mean. Is it something more on a feeling level than an intellectual one? Do you mean a listening that reaches out empathically - a type of active attunement or rapport?

T: This 'non-representational anticipation' might also bear some relation to what counsellors and psychologists would call 'free floating attention', or to the psychoanalytic method of 'free association'.

R: Terms such as 'empathic listening' or 'free-floating association' may indeed point to something akin to non-representational anticipation. But by simply reformulating Heidegger's message in these established terms, we run the risk of reducing it to something already familiar rather than bringing into view something as yet 'un-heard-of'.

T: And that is precisely the danger of representational thinking. For by representing someone's meaning in comfortable, familiar terms, we assume without further ado that we have 'heard' or 'understood' their message.

R: Not only that. We also assume, without any further ado, that the terms themselves are self-explanatory - that we know with absolute certainty what they mean. In this case what the terms 'empathic listening', 'rapport' or 'free-floating attention' mean.

S: We might certainly discuss what these terms mean to us. And they are, I suppose, psychological terms as opposed to philosophical or 'ontological' ones. But how do Heidegger's ontological terms such as 'being', 'being there' and 'being with' help us? How do they bring us closer to understanding the real nature of psychotherapeutic or psychoanalytic listening?

T: Surely, that is an important question. After all, isn't there also a danger that a Heideggerian approach to therapy will simply substitute esoteric philosophical language for existing psychoanalytic languages - some of which are quite esoteric enough? Or else that it replaces everyday concepts and 'representations' - which people can at least make sense of - with obscure ontological concepts which elude and mystify them. Better the devil you know...

R: You are certainly right in highlighting the contrast between ontological discourse on the one hand, and, on the other hand, either everyday terms or psychoanalytic discourse. But I would not dismiss the value of ontology so lightly. We have already a historic example of the immense and challenging impact that it can have on counselling and therapy - not through the substitution of one set of terms or one theory for another - but by raising questions to do with the fundamental inner stance of the listener.

S: To what... or whom... are you referring?

R: To Martin Buber, whose distinction between the 'I-Thou' and 'I-It' relation has had great impact on the helping professions, and who was a great influence on Carl Rogers. One might also mention Abraham Maslow, one of the principal founders of humanistic psychology, but one whose writing on the ''Psychology of Being' reveals that in essence his thinking was *ontological* rather than purely 'psychological'.

T: I must say I find it curious - if not dubious - that you call Buber and Maslow to the defence of Heidegger. Buber - a Jewish thinker, and Maslow a humanistic one. Surely we all know too well of Heidegger's notorious period of involvement with National Socialism - not to mention his explicit rejection of humanism. Buber's philosophy dealt above all with the ethical and relational dimension of the human being. We know that Heidegger had little to say on ethics, and that Buber himself accused him of reducing authentic human relating to mere 'care' or 'solicitude' for others.

R: To begin with, let us remind ourselves of just one thing. Nazi ideology was the application of a biological 'medical model' to the ills of society - with the Jews and others cast as foreign bodies comparable to a 'bad' gene, virus or cancer in need of extermination. At the same time no thinker has done more to undermine the foundations of racial-biological ideology, not to mention biological and (eu-)genetic medicine and psychiatry, than Martin Heidegger. That is not to say that the questions you have raised in your last statement can be lightly dismissed. Nor can they be lightly answered, as many would believe. Instead they remain largely unexplored. Nevertheless they are important questions, which have a particular personal meaning for me and, I believe, a larger social and historic significance. This larger significance lies in the fact that neither before or after the Holocaust was it seen as 'politically correct' - dare I say 'racially correct' - to seek a philosophical marriage of German and Jewish thinking and thinkers. As if the only outcome of such a marriage would be a race-philosophical mongrel of 'mixed blood'. The fact is of course that no face-to-face encounter and no full-blooded philosophical dialogue took place between Heidegger and Buber. All that we know of is a one-sided critical sally against Heidegger from Buber and an indirect and critical reference to Buber's 'I and Thou' from Heidegger. That makes it all the more important that the dialogue be pursued by others - that the deep inner relation between Buber's 'ethical' or 'relational ontology' and Heidegger's 'fundamental ontology' should not remain 'un-theme' in philosophy. For their respective ways of thinking do not merely contrast with but complement and enrich one another in the most philosophically and ethically significant ways.

S: I was interested to hear what you said about Maslow. But why do you see a 'synthesis' of Heidegger and Buber as so important?

R: Alone, but above all also together, they offer important keys to an 'ontology' of listening and to a recognition of its centrality to both thinking and the inter-human.

T: I agree that what you say is very interesting indeed, but it brings a great many questions to my mind and requires, I think, quite a bit of evidence and explication to support it.

R: Perhaps we can hear your questions one by one.

T: Well, to begin with, what has our earlier discussion of representational and non-representational listening to do with Buber?

R: What Heidegger called representational thinking is exactly what is involved in what Buber referred to as the 'I-It' way of relating to others. To put it more bluntly, where there is interpretation - or representation of any sort - there is no true 'I-You' relation in Buber's sense.

S: But surely if that's the case, nobody relates 'authentically' to anyone. After all, we all have thoughts about one another and in this way interpret and represent each other's words and behaviour.

R: That may be so. The question is, do we also relate to the other person as a being - not only as an object of the thoughts or feelings we have 'about' them? To quote Buber: 'Becoming 'I', I say You.' Only by being fully present to ourselves as beings - only as an 'I' in Buber's sense - can we relate to the other person as a being - as a 'You'.

T: That may indeed be the essence of Buber's message concerning the 'I-You' relation, hackneyed though this phrase has now become. But where, for God's sake, do you find any echo of it in Heidegger, save, as Buber complained, in the more impoverished attitude of mere 'solicitude' for others? For that matter, where do you find God in Heidegger - or what you call the inner You?

R: Heidegger recognised very well that we are not beings who just happen to 'have' relationships. We are relational beings. To be is to relate - both to other human beings and to our own inner being (the inner You). Then again there is our potential to relate to the inner being of others directly from our own inner being. This potentiality was what Heidegger termed a *Thou-Thou* (Du-Du) relationship as opposed to Buber's 'I-You' (Ich-Du) or 'I-Thou' relationship. Only in this way can we also come to truly 'know' the other. For as Heidegger emphasised: 'The relation that distinguishes knowing is always the one in which *we* ourselves are related and in which the relation vibrates throughout our basic posture.' The same message is echoed in his profound saying concerning the essential nature of listening: '*We* hear, not the ear.' Let us heed this saying thoroughly, letting it resound through different pronouns. Instead of Heidegger's 'we' let us say '*I* hear, not my ear'. Then we can begin to hear the misplaced intonation in the hackneyed phrase 'I *hear* you'. For I *hear* you only if there is a real sense in which I hear *you* and not merely your words or voice. I hear You only if it is *I* that hear you and not just my ears. For when *I* hear you I am all ear, I listen with and from my whole being and can therefore hear a being - hear *you* and not just *hear* you.

S: But instead of talking about 'listening with one's whole being', why can't we simply talk about giving someone one's wholehearted attention?

R: For one thing, because to listen with one's 'whole heart' is no more to listen with one's whole being than to listen with one's 'whole head' or 'whole mind'. And secondly, because 'attention' is something we give to something - to a word or gesture, a tone of voice or expression, a thought or feeling. It is a mode of outward relation to something - even to inner 'things' such as feelings or thoughts. We attend to an 'It' in Buber's sense. A 'You' is not some 'thing' we can attend to, but a being we must actively *intend* - with and from our whole being.

T: Your distinction between attention and intention is an intriguing reformulation of Buber. If I understand you correctly, we attend to some-thing, an 'It', but we intend some-one - a You. And yet surely we intend things too. Are not all objects of consciousness also intentional objects?

R: To intend something in the sense I am calling on is to truly mean it as a being. So long as something - or somebody - is merely an object of our scrutiny or manipulation, its beingness evades us, nor do we really mean or intend it with our whole being. Buber's 'I-You' relation can be understood also in a Heideggerian way: relating to a thing - an 'It' - in its beingness, and not merely as an object.

S: I still don't see how such philosophical distinctions, however 'ontologically' fundamental they may be, can be made tangible and meaningful in the inter-personal realm, and specifically in the realm of psychotherapy training.

R: Your question is a pertinent one, all the more so because the approach to listening that I am seeking to describe does not itself derive from an impersonal theoretical construct or technical skill. Instead it is more like an inner stance or bearing - one that is cultivated in our inner being and embodied in silence, not something that stems from without and needs then to be internalised like a theory or technique.

T: You seem then to be admitting that this inner bearing is so complex and esoteric that only the few can understand and cultivate it.

R: Rather, it is something so essentially simple and familiar to the many that the few fail to acknowledge its theoretical significance, and the many fail to cherish and cultivate it in everyday life.

S: But if you have no other way - besides these cryptic words - of explaining what you are referring to, how does your answer help us?

R: I have already said that the stance I am referring to is one to be embodied rather than turned into an abstract intellectual theory or applied technique. But if you will permit a small experiment, perhaps your question can be answered in a wordless and yet more tangible and concrete way.

S: By all means.

R: Look at my eyes. Observe and note their shape, colour and movement.

S: O.K.

[silent pause]

R: Now look at my eyes again. But this time with the intent to be fully there as an 'I' in your eyes, and to really see ME and not just my eyes.

S: All right

[longer, more pregnant pause]

R: Now, was there a difference?

S: Of course there was. When you asked me to look at you we made real contact. More than that. I sensed a lot of silent communication going on through this contact. But what are you getting at with this experiment?

R: Precisely that this contact and communication came about when you ceased to regard my eyes as a physical object of perceptual scrutiny.

T: Ah! Now I see what you are getting at. It reminds me of an article I once read by John Heron on the phenomenology of the social encounter, in particular the human gaze. His arguments were directed against those who thought this sort of silent eye contact communication could be explained by the fact that we constantly 'read' people's 'body language' including their eye signals. What he and you are suggesting is almost the opposite of this position. To paraphrase what you said before: Where communication depends on an interpretation or 'reading' of other people's words or body signals there is no real relation.

R: Indeed, for how else are we to explain the fact that experience of real inner contact through the gaze only comes about when you stop looking at someone's eyes and cease turning them into a sign - a mere object of scrutiny and interpretation.

S: This helps me understand your distinction between attention and intention. When you said 'now look at me' I engaged in an 'intentional act' of a quite different sort to the one I engaged in when you told me to look at your eyes and examine them.

R: Can you say more about this difference?

S: It's very difficult to describe. I suppose, however that the best way of naming it is to echo Buber's language and to say that in some way I became more fully embodied and present to myself as an 'I' and at the same time in deeper contact with you.

T: Which is to say in embodying your 'I' you were able to truly intend another being - a 'You' - rather than simply attending to them.

S: But now we seem to have left the realm of listening and hearing altogether and instead entered the realm of the optical, of vision and gaze. Are you suggesting that there is some equivalent of eye contact in the realm of listening?

R: I would suggest that listening is the intentional direction of an inner gaze, indeed essentially the same inner gaze that is communicated through the eyes - the gaze of our meaningful intent.

T: But how can this lead to the same experience of inner contact and communication as eye-contact can? After all, the latter is conditional upon a mutual gaze. People can look at one another at the same time but how can they possibly listen to one another at the same time?

R: If you would permit me another phenomenological experiment.

T: Certainly.

R: Then place your hand on mine and feel its surface and contours, its flesh and bones.

[silent pause]

R: All, right. Now withdraw your hand.

T: O.K.

R: Now place your hand on mine again. But this time with the intent to really touch ME and not just my hand.

[longer, more pregnant pause]

[R: slowly withdraws his hand from the contact]

T: Mmm. I can only echo what has already been said about the difference between making genuine eye contact and studying someone's eyes or eye signals.

R: Namely?

T: That in responding to your request to touch You - as opposed merely to feeling your hand - I was called upon to somehow summon and gather this 'I', to summon my whole being or inner self. And yet this makes it sound too much like a purely inward process, for my intent was above all to fully embody this 'self' in my touch.

R: And through your hand to embody your intent to touch me in my being.

T: I must say it was quite a simple but powerful and stretching exercise.

R: It is interesting to note that the words tend, tendril, tension, attend and intend all derive from the Latin *tendere* - to stretch or 'span'.

T: The word 'tension' makes sense here, for I felt half-way between relaxation and anxiety - a sort of subtle tensioning of my whole being.

R: ...as you sought to span the distance between one being and another, to stretch out a tendril of intent....

S: ...and as a result experienced the fundamental oscillation of true relation.

S: This is marvellously poetic, but how, if I may ask, does this answer the question about the lack of mutuality in listening?

R: Precisely in that the inner gaze of our listening intent has the character of an inner vibrational touch, a touch in which the listener is at the same time inwardly touched.

T: That is interesting. After all, we speak of being touched inwardly by someone's look or by their gaze. Why not by the 'inner gaze of their listening intent' as you call it? But isn't - if you will excuse the phrase - this 'touchy-feely' stuff more the domain of Humanistic, Gestalt or neo-Reichian psychotherapy? It certainly doesn't fit hand in hand with my image of Heidegger or Buber.

R: I understand your guardedness towards such exercises. But remember that their purpose was not to offer the intimacy of touch and the mutual gaze as substitutes for therapeutic listening, but rather to point to a type of listening which does not avoid the intimacy of authentic relation.

S: Are you suggesting that therapists in some way avoid intimate and authentic relation with their clients?

R: The problem is that in our culture, intimacy is identified with intimate talk or the intimacy of physical touch, with speech or sexuality, 'the word' or the 'the flesh' - but not with the intimacy of deep listening. The myth of our culture, therefore, is that intimate relating belongs only to the domain of intimate relationships; relationships forged through speech and embodied in sexuality.

T: Whereas what you are suggesting is what?

R: That it is not the way we speak with people or our physical closeness that determines the degree of intimacy with which we relate to them but the depth of our listening. Yet here we find evidence of a taboo no less strong than the nineteenth century sexual taboo.

S: What taboo is that?

R: The taboo against the intercourse of soul that arises when we listen intimately to others. For when *I* hear rather than my ear or my mind, and when I hear you - really mean you with my listening - then I also touch you with the inner gaze of my listening intent. This dimension of listening I call 'inner vibrational touch'.

T: It is interesting that when we speak of handling someone sensitively, we have in mind the words we use in addressing them, the tone of voice we adopt and the matters we raise. One talks of avoiding painful or 'touchy' subjects for example. We think only in terms of the sensitivity of our speaking and not the sensitivity of our listening and its wordless and bodiless touch - this 'inner vibrational touch'. But what sort of touch is this?

R: In listening we touch the other not with the physical body that speaks and gestures, but with our relational body - what I call our 'listening body'.

T: Now you seem to be getting even further from Heidegger and Buber. Next you'll be speaking, like Rudolf Steiner and the anthroposophists, about 'astral' and 'etheric' bodies.

R: Steiner's 'spiritual science' contains, I believe, a serious and rich phenomenology of bodyhood that deserves study from all students of Heidegger. For the nature of bodyhood was an issue that Heidegger recognised as the final, beckoning and most challenging frontier of his work. An issue addressed in the Zollikon seminars organised for doctors and psychiatrists by Medard Boss.

S: But surely the bodily and sexual dimensions of human language and relating are something that has already been recognised and explored in psychoanalysis?

R: And yet it stays within the exclusive domains of language and sexuality, the Word and the Flesh, mind and body.

S: Instead of what ... ?

R: Instead of admitting the soul and exploring the intercourse of soul that listening draws us into.

S: What you call 'inner vibrational touch'. But what do you mean by 'soul'?

R: The answer to your question lies in the question itself. Whenever we ask 'what do you mean by....?' we imply that it is a 'you' - a being - who mean things. To ask about the meaning of the word 'soul' is therefore paradoxical. For only a *being who means* can mean something through this question, and something through the word 'soul'. By 'souls', therefore, I understand nothing more or less than beings who can mean or intend. A computer can calculate or show us information. A robot can imitate human actions. But neither means something - or means someone - when they do so. They are not beings who mean nor do they mean other beings.

T: But perhaps we could return to the theme of listening and therapy, and with it to the taboo you mentioned. In what way do you see Heidegger and Buber as having challenged the taboo on intimate listening, 'inner vibrational touch' and 'intercourse of soul' - and how is this relevant to therapy?

R: To quote Martin Buber, 'The sicknesses of the soul are sicknesses of relationship.' He understood the spirit relationally - as the inner relation of each being to its self-being. He understood the soul relationally - as the embodied relation of human beings to another and to their innermost being. Each in their own way, Heidegger and Buber both embodied a new 'inner bearing' of soul - a new inner relationship to language and being. They embodied and articulated new ways of listening to language and to other human beings, new ways of 'being in the world' and 'being with others'. Their soul bearing was expressed not only in their thinking and in their way of speaking but in the type of listening from which they drew their thoughts and their words - how they meant them and meant each other with them.

S: You are talking then about their character and personality as individuals, and not just their philosophical writings. What bearing do character and personality have on someone's listening?

R: An essential one, if, by personality, you mean the way an individual bears and bodies themselves forth in speech.

T: And by character ... ?

R: The way an individual bears and bodies themselves in silence.

S: And how does bearing relate to listening?

R: To listen is to 'bear with' another being in silence, to drop our masks or personae, our roles and agendas, our verbal clothing and camouflage - and simply be a body: some-body.

T: To embody who we are in silence.

R: Which means also to bear who we are in a bodily way and to embody who we are in our whole bearing.

T: And to relate to who others are.

R: To 're-late' in the original and essential sense of 'to bear back'. In listening we bear back what others bare to us and bear towards us.

T: But we bear this back in silence rather than in words. As an inward listening response.

R: Indeed so, for our words themselves will only ring with meaning if they resound with this inner listening response. This is a response that cannot be represented in words but which communicates directly and wordlessly from our inner being, not in the word but through it: dia-logos.

S: This sounds to me as if you are saying that listening is a mode of what Winnicott called 'direct' or 'silent' communication.

T: Whereas speech is a form of indirect communication in words and images - representations in your terms.

R: Or perhaps we could say that relating is direct, silent, embodied communication. Whereas communication is indirect, symbolic relating - a 'bearing back' in symbols or signals.

T: This would mean that relating is essentially bound up with character and with the character of our listening, the way we bear ourselves and bear with others in silence. So that the depth and maturity of character, as well as the depth and maturity of our thinking and speaking, are both linked to the depth and maturity of our listening and of our silence.

R: And communicated by the tone of that silence. Its depth and fullness.

T: You spoke before of listening as a mode of intent, a way of meaning someone. To intend, perhaps, is also to set a tone. Like the silent, inward intent of a master musician or singer - an intent which sets the tone and determines the tonality of their singing or playing.

R: Or like the intent of masters in musical listening, who not only allow the music to touch them but who echo and recreate its silent tones in their soul. Intention is also a silent inner tonation, the toning of an inner music.

T: What difference then do you see in the characteristic tone and intonation of Buber's and Heidegger's thinking - and listening - respectively.

R: For Buber, listening meant essential relation - listening to others and responding to the other as a You, a being. For Heidegger, it meant essential translation - listening to language and responding to what addresses us through it - letting language speak. Response in Buber takes the form of an ethical 'response-ability' to another being, not in words but silently and dialogically - 'through the word' rather than in it. Response in Heidegger takes the form of a mutual 'co-respondence' to language itself, and, through it, to the call of Being. For Buber a listening dialogue meant a direct relation of beings. For Heidegger, it meant a joint response to Being and its logos.

S: How are these positions to be reconciled?

R: Buber emphasised a listening attuned to the other in their essential being. And yet such an inner listening contact with another can only truly come about on the basis of a deep listening contact with ourselves, a refusal to overhear our own inner voice in our eagerness to hear the voice of the other. To listen with the inner or 'third' ear is to be 'all ears' - to listen with our whole being and not to listen away from ourselves. Similarly, to be fully with another in our listening is also to fully be with them - to be fully present in an embodied way.

T: But isn't there a danger of self-absorption in this listening posture?

R: Only if in being inwardly present to ourselves we do not at the same time lean or 'list' our inner being towards the inner being of the other. And yet the tension between the respective listening postures of Heidegger and Buber is nevertheless not one to be casually resolved. Rather listening itself is this tension or *Spannung* through which we 'span' the gap between our own self-being and the being of another. It remains true nevertheless, that if our listening is not grounded in an 'essential relation' to our own self-being we cannot establish an essential relation to others in their self-being.

S: Another way of putting it might be to say that we can make authentic contact with others only by making contact with the part of ourselves that *is* in contact with them - that is genuinely *with* them.

R: Except that as long as it is not our whole being but just a 'part' of ourselves that constitutes this bridge between ourselves and others, we remain a-part from ourselves and the other.

S: Though perhaps it is the very pain of this a-partness that calls us back to ourselves, allowing us to re-link ourselves with our inner being and thereby establish an inner listening connection with another person.

R: Only if this pain of a-partness that you speak of is not emotionalised or covered up in superficiality - not 'expressed' or ''repressed' but instead felt and embodied.

T: What does it mean to 'embody' a feeling rather than to experience it as a labelled emotion that is to be expressed or repressed?

R: Precisely to *feel* that feeling in a bodily way rather than reflecting on it in one's mind - and to actively body that feeling through one's entire bodily demeanour. The art of communicating feelings through one's bodily demeanour is something that has been sacrificed on the altar both of psychoanalysis and psychotherapy - where the intrinsic *meaning* of bodily *de-meanour* is denied,.

T: Instead of which a person's demeanour is thought of as something in need of interpretation - seen as a signifier of some sort of unspoken *verbal* message.

S: In which case the whole idea of *body* language is emptied of meaning and reduced to body *language* - seen as a vehicle for the expression of meanings which are essentially verbal rather than bodily. Whereas in actuality what communicates through bodily demeanour is precisely what can only be meant 'through the word' - and not in any way represented in words.

T: That makes me think of the way parents often tell children not to frown or sulk - or generally demand verbal explanations when they receive an unwelcome message from a child's demeanour.

S: Not because they don't understand the message but because they do.

T: But instead of responding to the child's demeanour 'through the word' themselves - responding to the child sensitively through their own demeanour - they put pressure on the child to alter their demeanour, or even worse, to verbalise their emotions in an 'adult' way.

S: If I understand this correctly then, the whole Freudian and post-Freudian notion that it is only through language that the unconscious is made conscious is questionable. For it assumes that we cannot consciously become aware of our feelings in a bodily way and consciously communicate them through our demeanour.

R: What is called the 'talking cure' can too easily become a cure that evades the pain of heeding a wordless and embodied message and taking it to heart - responding to others *from* one's feelings rather than talking 'about' them.

S: The pain of being a body rather than a talking head.

R: And of being with some-body in a bodily way.

S: Rather than in a detached and dispassionate or passionate and expressive way.

T: But isn't emotional self-expression also something bodily - a form of physical movement and bio-energetic release?

R: The concept of emotional expression implies that feelings are things we 'have' inside us. It leads us to translate what goes on *between* people into some 'thing' going on 'inside' them. It turns the human qualities they embody in their way of relating to others - in their demeanour - into internal objects of mutual self-reflection. It turns something we *do* - feeling - into 'feelings' that we have. As a result people cease to listen and relate to one another in an embodied way - to experience listening as a way of directly and wordlessly feeling themselves and feeling the other. Instead they talk in a disembodied way 'about' their own or other people's labelled emotional feelings. What Heidegger called 'steadfast' hearing (*standhaltendes Hören*) is a grounded and embodied way of listening, a way of listening that calls upon us to take a stand 'under' all this talking about.

S: And through this, to really 'under-stand' each other, to truly feel the other.

T: But doesn't this supposedly mature form of listening come very close to adopting a merely unemotional posture - to being so 'centred' that we are stoically unmoved by other people's feelings?

R: On the contrary, it is through pre-maturely giving expression to our emotional responses that we resist letting be what really moves us, preventing it from oscillating in the deepest centres of our listening body and coming to rest there. Or rather, we prevent what moves us from coming to rest where it most essentially belongs - not 'in' me or in the other person but in the oscillating 'between'. A steadfast hearing is a hearing (*zu-hören*) that belongs to (*gehört zu*) this Between.

T: Not a hearing that appropriates its contents as private emotional property or treats them as the private emotional property of the other.

S: From whence comes the psychoanalytic discourse regarding the 'transference' or 'projection' of such emotional private property from one to the other.

R: We are speaking instead of a Gelassenheit or 'letting be' that lets be what gathers in 'the between'.

S: And thus lets it speak in the mode of silence. This is, I suppose, what Heraclitus meant by listening to the *logos* of the *psyche* - to the wordless gathering of meaning within and between beings.

[silence]

R: When beings gather, Being gathers.

[silence]

T: I fear that we have come a long way again from the day-to-day work of therapists. Our dialogue seems very much in tune with Heidegger's statement 'Man speaks in the mode of silence'. But where does this leave the role of verbal intervention and response in the therapeutic dialogue?

S: I find myself in agreement with this question. At what stage does it become appropriate for the therapist to respond verbally to a client, as well as through inner listening contact and communication?

R: This question is indeed one for each therapist to ponder. One could go further and argue that the way an individual therapist *times* their therapeutic response, defines their way of giving therapy and determines the quality depth of their response.

S: Does the question then lead us then into the realm of *Being and Time* and their inner relation?

R: It certainly leads us to consider the fundamental relation of *Being and Listening* on the one hand, and of *Listening and Time*, on the other. For we are speaking of the *qualitative depth* of the time that the therapist grants to a client, and perhaps also of the essence of listening itself as a qualitative inward expansion of time - something quite different from the measurable time boundaries of a therapy session or the measurable time or 'turn' interval between address and response in the therapeutic dialogue.

T: How then would a therapist who adopts the philosophical listening stance that you have discussed with us answer the question? How would they time their spoken interventions?

R: Remember first the statement of Heidegger's you referred us to. He did not say man remains silent and then speaks. He said man speaks in the mode of silence.

S: Presumably this is not a reference to what is called 'inner speech' - something which in this context would refer to the inwardly verbalised thoughts and mentally spoken words that go through a therapist's mind as they listen?

R: Indeed not. For these inner voices do not themselves speak in the mode of silence. They are themselves interpretations of the therapist's own wordless inner response to the client - interpretations of the inner voice that speaks in the mode of silence.

T: I believe you have argued elsewhere that this inner voice communicates automatically and directly to the client, even if it is not translated in words.

R: That's right.

T: But what if I sense angry, judgmental voices in me. Will not these too, communicate directly to the client? Is it not dishonest and unauthentic to keep silent about my own anger?

R: Here we touch upon the question of emotions again. The point is not to either express or repress such inner voices and the emotions they express but to be in touch with the wordless feeling tones that they themselves translate into inner speech.

S: You mean I suppose, to listen to them - much as we listen to the various voices of the client.

R: Something we can only do if we neither identify with them nor disidentify from them.

R: Both of which prevent us from really hearing them and heeding what they tell us.

T: This sounds fine, but it only defers the question I raised earlier - as to how and when it becomes appropriate to actually open our mouths and offer verbal feedback to the client, rather than engaging in prolonged introspective audition of our own inner voices - not to mention the many voices of the client.

S: What is your answer to this question?

T: Personally, I delay response until I have some sort of gut feeling or reaction to a client's words.

S: That means giving their words time to 'sink in'

R: A phrase that reminds us that listening is not something we do only while someone is speaking but also after they have spoken. But this is only possible if the listener exercises the basic discipline of restraint or *Verhaltenheit* that Heidegger spoke of: a withholding of immediate verbal response. Only this basic discipline can prevent dialogue degenerating into idle talk or argumentation - a mere mutual exchange of thoughtless, emotionally reactive or intellectually defensive responses. It is only restraint of withholding that prevents us from seeking to deflect the word of the other with our own and instead allows it to 'sink in' as you say.

S: 'Withholding' then, is not just a guarantee that we fully 'hear someone out' rather than prematurely interrupting them. It grants time for us to not only hear but *heed* their words themselves - to let their deeper inner sense 'get under our skin', penetrate our verbal defences and resonate within us.

T: Then do 'heeding' and 'letting resonate' mean simply letting ourselves be touched in a gut way and then responding from gut feeling?

R: Not if this implies that 'gut feeling' is not itself something we need to first withhold, heed and let resonate within us. The voice of 'gut feeling' is all too often the reactive or defensive expression of an already familiar voice within us - one so loud we do not even bother to listen to it before giving voice to it. 'Letting resonate' on the other hand, means hearing the word of the other as the echo of an as-yet unheard and unfamiliar voice within us. It is that voice, *hidden* within 'gut feeling' which we must *heed*.

S: So that in heeding we listen beneath and beyond the division between our own 'inner voices' and the thoughts and feelings voiced by the client.

R: The words in which clients express themselves always mean more than the thoughts and feelings they communicate. They do not just communicate the private psychic world of the client, nor are they a mere mirror of the therapist's projective interpretations. They bespeak 'the between' - 'We-meanings' as well as 'my' meanings or 'your' meanings, 'I-meanings' or 'You- meanings'.

T: How does 'withholding' help the therapist to hear someone's words as an expression of these 'we' meanings?

R: What is most meaningful in the word only reaches us in the silence that follows speech. Only by *withholding* can we *hold* to a client's words as words and let them speak to us. For to let words speak to us means not simply registering a gut reaction but asking ourselves what as yet unheard voice they communicate. It means giving them a 'second hearing', one in which we let a phrase spoken by another linger and echo within us - hearing it in the precise manner and with the precise wording in which it was uttered. By letting the words of another echo and resound in us in this way, we can begin to feel their wordless inner sense or *resonance*.

S: I recall that at the beginning of our discussion we defined listening as a type of wordless, non-representational anticipation or precognition of what there is to be said. Now you seem to be suggesting that another part of listening is also a precise recollection of the exact words and tone of voice in which something has been said.

R: These two aspects of deep listening are precisely what reveals its essence as a mode of direct non-representational knowing or cognition. Deep listening is both a pre- and a post-cognition of the spoken word. It was the lack of such a listening that Heraclitus pointed to when he described the word or *logos* of the *psyche* as that which 'men fail to comprehend both before hearing it and once they have heard.'

T: Here again I am slightly confused, though. What is the nature of this 'non-representational' recollection of what has been said? If we do not represent to ourselves what has been communicated to us in *words*, then how are we to recollect it at all, save perhaps as a gut reaction or feeling?

R: There is a world of difference between recollecting through *representing* and recollecting through *letting resonate*. To recollect another person's meaning by *representing* them in our own words is by no means the same as letting *their* words echo and resonate within us. The inner sense of a word is its inner resonance. Conversely, only out of the inner resonance of the word can its deeper inner sense come to light.

T: You mean that simply letting another person's words echo within us is all that is necessary to come to an intuition or insight of what they are saying.

R: 'Intuition' and 'insight' are words with the same root meaning: to bring something into view or behold it before our inner eye.

S: Then letting resonate is perhaps the link between *withholding*, holding to the word of the other - letting it resonate - and quite literally *beholding* deeper levels of meaning. A link, in other words, between inner listening and inner seeing or 'in-sight'.

R: I would suggest that the *be-holding* that follows from the exercise of *withholding* does indeed have the character of an inner seeing.

S: But if this seeing takes the form of visual images is this not equally a mere form of representational thinking?

R: Only if it takes the form of a seeing with which one seeks to pictorially represent in some way the given or *literal* meaning of words. This is what I call the linguistic imagination - made up of fixed and stereotyped word-images. In contrast to this type of 'seeing' is what I call the *listening imagination.* The listening imagination is a *feeling seeing,* in which, as in our dreams, mental images serve as imaginative *metaphors* of wordlessly *fel*t meanings and comprehensions.

T: Are you speaking of a type of dreamlike, clairvoyant imagination? A sort of second sight?

R: A 'second sight' that only emerges from giving ourselves the opportunity to truly heed someone's word and give them a 'second, hearing' - one in which we *feel* for the inner sense and resonance of their words.

S: And in that way come to have 'second thoughts' about what someone has said - second thoughts that first take the form both of directly *felt* comprehensions and of imaginative metaphorical insights that give these comprehensions form.

R: It is precisely such 'second' thoughts that belong to the essence of thinking itself in the way that Heidegger described it, as 'a listening which brings something to view'.

T: This is beginning to make sense to me now. For it is often only some time after a client has left the consulting room that I begin to *feel* the meaning of their words and of their entire comportment from *within* myself. It is then also that deeper 'in-sight' might emerge into something they said, perhaps just a single word or phrase that now strikes me as having borne a deeper meaning.

S: A word or phrase that you no doubt thought you understood when you first heard it, but only because you had not yet had time to suspend your ordinary linguistic understanding and give it second thought - a second, more inward hearing.

R: So long as we are wrapped up in listening to words we have not yet heard those words. For we have not yet seen into the word.

T: And yet the insight that I gain through this second hearing is like hearing for the first time, for it links particular words and phrases with otherwise formless but felt impressions that I had all the while.

R: The word now impresses you as the bearer of something which it bore all along but which required time to come to birth within you. And yet the paradox is that this second hearing and second sight is indeed a relaxed and inwardly focused hearing and sight. It is not the result of any sort of straining to empathise with or see into or see through the client.

T: It is probably this sort of straining you refer to that prevents such insights from emerging during sessions themselves.

R: The listening imagination is a visioning of the inner states and outer events to which they themselves are responding, and of which they form a part.

S: Strange indeed that in one's desire to respond to the words and actions of others one forgets that these are already a response to something else.

T: So if I understand you correctly, the listening imagination is a way of visioning the life-world to which the client is responding and visioning the client in this world. Not a verbal response to the client but a feeling in-sight into that which moves the client to speak in the first place.

S: Because only through a second, inward hearing can we attune directly to the world of which they speak and the words in which they speak of it - a world, in relation to which all words they speak to us are merely an indirect response. Giving someone a second hearing after they have spoken means giving ourselves the chance to have second thoughts about what we have heard - and in this way to think the as yet unheard.

R: And yet in my experience the second hearing that leads to insight can itself be deepened by 'second sight' that precedes it. By this I mean the ability to not simply visualise the life-world of the client as they describe it in words but to take a mental 'snapshot' of the face and body of the client as they speak. Holding to and beholding this mental after-image of the body of the client is a quite different mode of 'second sight'.

T: What is the advantage to be gained from attending to this mental after-image of the client's face and body rather than just observing it directly with one's own body?

R: The advantage lies in being able to then inwardly feel one's way *into* the after-image, and in this way gain a direct felt sense of the inner states of being that person's demeanour embodies.

T: That is most interesting, for sometimes when a client has left my consulting room I find myself left with a vague residual *feel* of the whole mood of their embodied presence - something I feel in my own body.

R: The trick is then to give form to this residual bodily sense of a client's overall mood or feeling tone through second hearing and second sight. The second hearing involves letting particular words or phrases continue to resound within you as an 'after-echo'. The second sight means *also* holding a mental after-image of particular postures they adopt and of particular looks you have observed on their face and in their eyes.

T: But what is the particular significance of this form of second sight as opposed to second hearing?

R: It significance lies in the fact that what we are questing is an inner understanding of the outer human being - in particular a felt, bodily sense of the meaning of their outward bodily demeanour. A look in someone's eyes is no mere form of bodily or emotional self-expression. It reveals in a direct bodily way a person's whole way of looking out at, seeing and feeling and being in the world around them.

S: What you seem to be saying is that there is a whole lot more to so-called body language or demeanour than just bodily self-expression. And that in particular a person's 'way of looking at things' and their 'way of seeing things' is no mere mindset or collection of ideas but something quite directly embodied in the look in their eyes.

R: Exactly so. Philosophy and science have yet to grasp the full momentousness and magnitude of this inner relation between what we call 'mind' and what we call 'body'. For what philosophy has always considered simply as 'ideas' in the mind are essentially what in ordinary language we call 'ways of looking at things'. The looks on someone's face and in their eyes however, are a direct bodily revelation of an individual's way of looking at things - and of seeing and feeling them.

S: But what, I wonder, is the essential link between second hearing, second sight, and second thoughts?

T: Or between withholding, holding to someone's words and be-holding the inner states of being and outer life-world to which they are responding?

R: I would suggest that it is questioning. A questioning that has its source in a quest to feel the inwardness of another human being within oneself. A quest that demands also that we hold open questions within ourselves and feel those questions rather than seeking verbal answers to them from others. That we seek ways of directly experiencing the felt questions of others. For it is only when the listener is able to genuinely hold their own questions open and feel those questions within themselves that their listening becomes a fertile womb of listening in-sight.

S: I believe it was the psychoanalyst Robert Langs who suggested that therapists ask their questions silently rather than putting them to the client in words.

T: I have often noticed that in this way the client is *more* likely to respond authentically to these questions than when verbally challenged to produce answers to them.

S: The paradox is that being directly challenged to respond to a question verbally can positively encourage a veiled or inauthentic response - saying what the therapist wants to hear.

R: And only by withholding our verbal questions do we affirm our questions as shared questions of human being. These are questions that can only be felt in the realm of 'the between' - of human 'inter-being'.

S: A realm of inter-being which then brings the client closer to their own 'intra-being'. A withholding that helps the client to hear and hold to their own inwardly felt questions - to be and bear with them.

R: It is in this way that the client learns to validate their questions *as* questions, and not just as problems to be solved. Above all, it is in this way that they learn what it means to be and bear with a question in pregnant silence - to *listen*.

S: It seems, on second thoughts then, that listening and questioning are not two different things at all. Yet people tend to always identify questioning with putting verbally formulated questions to themselves or others.

T: And many therapists still understand dialogue as an alternation of verbal address and response, verbal questions and answers.

S: Rather than as a mutual quest of human beings for inner contact and relation, meaning and fulfilment.

C. Not in the word but through it.

R: As a wordless questing that is the very essence of listening.

S: A questing that hears the word as the communication of a silent quest.

R: And follows it deeper into the silence from whence it arises.

S: Allowing us to be the question rather than to speak it.

T: To embody it in our bearing and bear it back through our demeanour.

S: To hold it with the questioner.

T: And thereby behold it as a shared question.

R: A question of being.

T: To which both the thoughts and feelings of the client, and those of the therapist are a response - and a co-respondence.

R: The task of therapeutic listening is to behold this correspondence.

T: Which often appears as a synchronicity between the issues that a client brings to therapy and those experienced by the therapist in their own life.

S: One which is usually regarded either as merely co-incidental or a product of transference or projection.

T: Rather than part of the very nature of human communication and relating.

R: As the bearing back of a message that bespeaks a common quest.

S: A common quest that each individual translates into their own unique life language. What you have called their individual 'language of being'.

T: And translates too, into an existential language - their everyday way of being-in-the-world.

R: The events and phenomena they experience in their everyday world being themselves experiential 'words' - an expression of the experiential language through which they *world* their own being.

T: And through which their being nevertheless speaks in its own unique idiom.

S: In response to what addresses them through the 'word' of their experiential world.

R: Not a closed world of material bodies in space and time but of beings who body - and in their bodying, matter to one another.

S: Mattering being the same as meaning something to another being.

R: Something only possible if we each learn to authentically body our own innermost being in relating to all other beings.

S: And in that way restore our relationship to Being.

T: Leaving I suppose, the first and last word to let resonate in this listening dialogue between *Therapy and Philosophy* with Martin Heidegger himself...

MH: 'You cannot heal a single human being, even with psychotherapy, if you do not first restore his relationship to Being.'

R: For when beings gather, Being gathers.

S: Thus 'appropriating' beings unto itself in the manner that Heidegger named with the word *er-eignen*.

R: The 'coming into their own' of beings through a renewed sense of their mutual belonging to Being.

S: A belonging-together (*Zu-gehörigkeit*) of beings to one another and to Being which is essentially grounded in their hearing (*Gehör*) .

R: ...as an obedience (*Gehorsamkeit*) to that which calls to them from within and beyond themselves - and to which their listening (*Zuhören*) is itself a response.

T: A listening that requires more than just ears.

R: For as Heidegger emphasised: '*We* hear, not the ear.'

Bibliography

Buber, Martin *Eclipse of God* Humanities Press International 1988
Buber, Martin *I and Thou* T&T Clark 1996
Buber, Martin *On Intersubjectivity and Cultural Creativity* University of Chicago Press 1992
Castaneda, Carlos *The Power of Silence* Black Swan 1989
Fiumara, Gemma C. *The Other Side of Language; A Philosophy of Listening* Routledge 1990
Fox, Mathew *Meditations with Meister Eckhart* Bear and Company 1983
Frankl, Victor *The Will to Meaning* Touchstone 1984
Garfinkel, Harold *Studies in Ethnomethodology* Polity Press 2002
Gendlin, Eugene *Focusing* Bantam 1979
Gendlin, Eugene *Focusing-oriented Psychotherapy* Guilford Press 1996
Gendlin, Eugene *Experiencing and the Creation of Meaning* Northwestern University Press 1997
Goldstein, Kurt *The Organism* Zone Books 1995
Gordon, Paul *Face to Face; Therapy as Ethics* Constable and Company Ltd. 1999
Heidegger, Martin *Basic Questions of Philosophy* Indiana University Press 1994
Heidegger, Martin *Contributions to Philosophy* trans. Emad and Maly; Indiana University Press 1999
Heidegger, Martin *Poetry, Language, Thought* HarperCollins 1975
Heidegger, Martin *The Fundamental Concepts of Metaphysics* Indiana 1995
Heidegger, Martin *The Principle of Reason* Indiana University Press 1996
Heidegger, Martin *The Question Concerning Technology* trans. Lovitt; Harper Torchbooks 1977
Heidegger, Martin *Zollikon Seminars* Northwestern University Press 2001
Heidegger, Martin *Zollikoner Seminare* Klostermann 1994
Kockelmanns, Joseph *Edmund Husserl's Phenomenology* Purdue University Press 1994
Lakoff and Johnson *Metaphors We Live By* University of Chicago Press 1980
Langs, Robert *The Listening Process* Jason Aronson 1978
Levin, David M. *The Body's Recollection of Being* Routledge 1985
Levin, David Michael *The Listening Self* Routledge 1989
Roberts, Jane *The Seth Material* Prentice-Hall 1970
Wilberg, Peter *Being and Listening* Third Ear Publications 1998
Wilberg, Peter *Deep Socialism* New Gnosis Publications 2003
Wilberg, Peter *Head, Heart and Hara* New Gnosis Publications 2003
Wilberg, Peter *From New Age to New Gnosis* New Gnosis Publications 2003

Wilberg, Peter *From Psychosomatics to Soma-semiotics* New Gnosis Publications 2004
Wilberg, Peter *The Therapist as Listener* New Gnosis Publications 2004
Wilberg, Peter *Heidegger, Medicine and 'Scientific Method'* New Gnosis Publications 2004
Wilberg, Peter *The Language of Listening*, Journal of the Society for Existential Analysis 3
Wilberg, Peter *Introduction to Maieutic Listening* Journal of the Society for Existential Analysis 8.1
Wilberg, Peter *Listening as Bodywork* Energy and Character, Journal of Biosynthesis 30/2
Wilberg, Peter *Organismic Ontology and Organismic Healing* Energy and Character 31/1
Winnicott, Donald. *The Maturational Process and the Facilitating Environment* Hogarth 1965
Winnicott, Donald *Playing and Reality* Routledge 1991
Winnicott, Donald *The Maturational Process and the Facilitating Environment* Hogarth 1965